FACTORIES AND CITIES

A Poem in Two Parts

By

Dale Jacobson

For Art
Great meeting
you at last!
Dale
2014

ISBN: 1-4033-6000-6 (e-book)
ISBN: 1-4033-6001-4 (Paperback)
ISBN: 1+4033-6002-2 (Dustjacket)

This book is printed on acid free paper.

1stBooks - rev. 12/27/02

Acknowledgments:

Parts of this poem have been published in *Another Chicago Magazine, Jazz,* and *Forkroads.* Red Dragonfly Press published the section from Part II, *Hunting My Home Town,* as a beautiful hand-produced edition in 1997.

For

Thomas McGrath

and

Meridel LeSueur

whose words ride the future

PART I

Every Emanative joy forbidden as a Crime:
And the Emanations buried alive in the earth with pomp of religion:
Inspiration deny'd; Genius forbidden by laws of punishment:
I saw terrified; I took the sighs & tears, & bitter groans:
I lifted them into my Furnaces; to form the spiritual sword.
That lays open the hidden heart: I drew forth the pang
Of sorrow red hot: I workd it on my resolute anvil

-Los in *Jerusalem*
-William Blake

I ventured to hint that the Company was run for profit.

-Marlow in *Heart of Darkness*
-Joseph Conrad

Dale Jacobson

I.

Between the wind and the dust,
Is there room for a poor man's life?

-Tu Fu

Dale Jacobson

1.

(workers descend)

Down the factory smokestack
a shaft brutal as a volcanic heart
strikes to the earth's core,
the geology of extinct nostalgias,
convulsions at the source of the day,
a terror of young cremated lions.

A glowing tree of fire and masonry,
into the blue cool dawn it billows
the specter from the deep centuries,
the incense of impotent rages,
resentments loose in the past, dark despairs—
and in its white furnace it incinerates further
whatever has been exhausted beyond
remembering itself—histories that fell
like residue from the pale hands of workers.

And into the dusk goes blazing
a heat that warms no one, another day
burned out at its center and the husk
is swept away toward western dust.

With gloves of cinder, with terrible lungs of smoke
and eyes red as molten steel, then workers
descend, go down to the ore of the earth,
the stolid silences of stone, hour of fossil—
in dreams descend to the pale portals
of sulfur, the sky laminations of autumns.

Dale Jacobson

Beneath the cities they wander,
with pale hands, eyes delirious as fluid fire,
with empty pale hands, without money
they kneel at the fires of their torment,
in the lapping flames of their devoured days
try to see who they are: the salt and sweat
of centuries written upon their foreheads.

2.

(primordial birth: a brief cinerama of history...)

The night was pre-seraphic, brutal,
a forest whose hidden choirs
sharpened their cries upon the moon's
cold implacable silence...

Beyond the deep listening of the camp,
the collapsing requiem of crackling wood
and flowing circle of conversational hands,
there!—
            the sequestral dark loomed up,
one living body with a thousand hungers,
satirical bark and whine of beasts,
shadows within shadows shifting,
the savage silver of the stream
a rippling riddle past the place where
teeth tore out the soft ore of a throat,
calls of night birds huge in the dark,
deep solitude of the owl opening
a tunnel of air into air into
the wide wilderness of the stars.

And the plains stretched away, unrolling
into themselves, their fatalities seen
in the sun curling around the bleached bone,
and the distance from the rain to the dry root...

They walked quietly, listened for the silhouette
rustling the changing shape of its wild clothes.

In that tribal hour, before the stars were named,
somehow, someone spoke, launched
the verb to flight, carved from need

7

the weapon of the word, sculpted it
into a pointed stone to command death
like a flying serpent's tooth—and summon
the sizzling riot of midday flies where
the putrescence of spilled guts clung to the sun.

In the twilight the dance of masks bloomed!

The communal mind dreamed. Word became
song—rhythms built rhythms of the beast dying
until the blood could be tasted on the spears
and alien shrieks tore the dark linens of the abyss!

* * * * *

They planted names along the trail
to trap the wild voices, those *other* ones,
but were themselves caught by language,
which had its own future fires (somewhere
in the long shadow of tomorrow atoms
would talk to each other and annihilate cities…)

Drums rumored through the foliage…
Armies fought to possess the horizons,
which only shifted further away…
Distances rang with the assault of metals
forged in the conflagration of the tribal spark!
Metal wounded metal, iron argued against iron…

  At the edge of a sleeping, smoking mirror,
  the passing eye caught and lost a glimpse
  of itself: like warped time, the shaman s vision
  opened upon the nightmare of history's
  blind labyrinth, where the poet's voice echoed…

They put stone upon stone, made their own caves.
They tamed fire like a bird that shed its light

upon the walls of fortresses that were not safe,
nor could save the hand that had learned to take.

   The eerie remote cries
   retreated to the brooding hills
   leaning against the dusk…

In taming the distance, they opened their own:
the night dreamed in deep wells
but the waters of the day were clear.

* * * * *

Faint shadows growing into the dusk—
trees opening their branches to the night,
pale lunar leaves…
                a ground transformed…

Someone took fire, tied it to a stick,
walked out into the dark, invented a road…

That's all that happened—the rest is history.

And then:
the next morning, in some further century,
the hooves of horses aroused the dust
like all dead wings thrown up from earth,
a tunnel of thunder expanding …

Fire conquered the wilderness,
but in the flames—
                a wedding with darkness,
the abandoned encampments of ash…

The past could not be vanquished, and
like the wind beyond the city pale, a cold
slouching animal, the shadow of ice moved …

9

Dale Jacobson

Merchants signed gold upon the touchstone,
dark mirror where the future was locked.

For the poor: small birds with skeletons
of moonlight came after dark to steal
the minutes. In the morning they found
their words had become thin as thirsty thistles…

Comets streaked over the night of empires,
the punctuations of catastrophe in the sky:
blood and more blood,
                              tumultuous fury,
insistence upon lethargic urgency,
falling out of its own color,
out of its own need,
                    never quotable,
                                        measureless…

Like the long hollow spine of the wind
breaking,
            like an emptiness seeking a word,
the whips fell,
                a dark electric jealousy,
a transonic muteness of power that made
the air hiss
                the whips fell
                              in sibilant laceration—
cracked!—
            the dead law of leather upon slaves…

Each day the voice of the rivers descended
into the hunting hour of nighthawks.

The stars, voyaging the centuries, held
the new age that had risen to touch them.

3.

(lost people)

Alien bodies rushing past alien bodies
while astronomers map the heavens
and the moon's Sea of Tranquility sleeps
through its reign of permanence—

Thousands, millions, like nomads, like hunters
blazing internally, roaming the streets, combing
the red hair of neon lights with eyelashes
rooted in night, while their feet remember
somewhere beneath concrete, the earth
in her nameless solitude survives all seasons...

Wanderers lost without language,
without tools,
                    hunting whatever
they can eat—give me your name
and I will give you mine—a word
to reveal a world—listening for
what food means, and labor, the day
from dawn to dusk or sadness to nightfall,
hungering for home: the homeless
to be known by evidence of distance,
descendants of the far tribe we all are...
(who can free the jailed timekeeper?)

Unknown,
            undiscovered,
                        anonymous among
the commotion,
            strangers among strangers
in the strange cities,
                        who watch the twilight

11

enter like hunger their souls, like an existential
executioner stealing all but the hardened words,
by installments stealing not time but its meanings,
not light but its soul of a world woven together,
leaving each day to fall into a hollow place
like the ocean wave collapses into its own shadow,
falls through the ghost of itself: strangers
in their native country feel their lives fall away,
their birthday cakes carried off on the backs
of luminous ants into those moody spaces
of alleyways that eat pieces of silence at a time:
parts of the body
                    disappearing: a leg,
a hand,
        half a face…
                        nightmare of the homeless…

Upon the brows of children asleep
the luminous wax of the moon drips
like a candelabrum in the eternal house.

4.

(questions)

No future in the restless wandering!
I've been to the far cities, but never escaped the century…
Where would you go, traveler of the traveled countries,
among what place names will you find your name?

All journeys mapping the fugitive home come
to the same end—
               or beginning…
                            The hollow years
put on the faces of the night stars, or the faces of
the poorest among us,
                  or the weather whose changes
mean nothing until the primal sea stops us amazed:
arrival at the coronation of water upon the horizon
like a war of solitude no one wins—perhaps the wind.

What is the city center, place where people
have learned to talk as though they knew answers,
as though they heard the muffled gossip of the dust
in a country whose flag flies over so much contention?—
The city endures itself: a construction of antique
and savage moonlight—
                    a stone and ferrous maze,
a puzzle,
          elegy of neon bleeding down walls towards
the gutters, an intimacy of impersonal doors…

You came out of the unknown, out of the silence,
they gave you a language and you expected
to be found and found only those also unknown
to each other, prisoners whose crime no one can
define, whose hands travel off searching the deserts,

and beneath your shoe's sole your own thin soul,
the sound of your footsteps grinding into futility
the wandering identity of the streets…

* * * * *

A moment within a moment, the city is pure potential
when the discourse of sparrows wakes the day
like tiny carpenters whose chirps build
the communal arch of the sun toward noon.

The city is revealed in the early washing blue
as if a child had lifted a hand free from dream
and freed this vision, this solid stillness of buildings,
steps, walkways, and plazas already worn from
the familiar feet of the weather and the people
who entered long ago through the rain, or
was it the mist of the sea that brought them forward,
before the names of nations ruled the world?…

Who are they—those who do the work, who work
the earth, who make the tools, who use them?
Nothing that prolongs the world pops out of thin air:
all is born of labor, only labor gives birth…
all born from physical fact to physical fate.

Even the feel of a worn brick is more than a suggestion—
it holds a history of being in its archeological tenure:
the hand of the brickmaker, his father's hand,
the far ocean, the collective hands of workers…

This clay has absorbed the soul of fire…

This earth has ripened by fusion with the sun.

Within this brick our lives are housed.

The wind has cooled it to survive the wind.

There is memory in this brick of the calluses it gave
the mason, the armor hands build out of themselves…

In this brick is silence that has hardened out of words
that were spoken not because they were clever
but because they were true—necessary words
to create this brick: words endure as this brick
endures against wind and time, against fatalities,
this brick that gives shelter like words give shelter.

Still, each night we enter a deep lake,
                                        the dark
of our own monsters,
                            worlds falling through worlds—
the history we made that unmakes us,
                                        the shadow
of ice like an animal circling our cities, the past
unvanquished, or the faces of ourselves we meet
or fear meeting,
                        the poor always denied: our angers
become the grief of birds dreaming drowned tunnels,
we meet all the denied world of ourselves coming
and going we meet who we forgot and who
we will forget when we wake—
                                    who we failed
to become: and all the dark energies of worlds
calling invention—out of the ruined days…

                        * * * * *

And what were those cities, those walls
leaning against their own shadows,
anger or anguish raised brick by brick
in strict precision against the brutal light:
hierarchy of hierophants elevated to money-

15

heaven,
>   the one per cent who own the world
and ascend by crucifixion of the poor?

In the basements the boilers burned with a ferocity
that devoured anthracitic cemeteries of the eons!
All promises also thrown into the furnace,
day by day lost in smoke, except the long old,
cold one:
>   singular curse of labor:
>   exhaustion:
>   loss:

…stone, stone, and the tireless dead sung
into ultimate poverty through champagne and sun
that stung the ragged-raged eyes of the wronged
while sweat filled the rivers with stars,
and dream waters houred solitude to the sea…

5.

(west)

All the ancient and shattered gods eaten by the rain,
and immigrants with a portable holy ghost
journeying into the storms…
                            they went hunting
a home to plant their religion (what is the true God
without real estate?). They followed their shadows
by early day, by evening stretching them along—
transporting endurance, the hardest element on earth
forged in their hearts—they went west where
the morning star fades like a phantom, walked
the long road to the moon of the unknown,
and the wild night large as the call of crickets.

Called by land, by roots that drank the stars,
the loam their hands understood, called by
rivers and homestead,
                         horizons and wild chance.

* * * * *

I invoke a swirling wind,
                         its voice picking up
the angers the dead took with them into
the dust—dark discontents my inheritance.

    Can you hear the night dew
    collecting on the picks, all the gold
    shipped east from California?

    Can you hear the feet distance devoured,
    those wanderers who dragged
    their shadows from deaf stone

17

to the river's falling word?

They wore the wind like tattered
dawns, immigrants from darkened
lands: sawyers, carpenters, forgers,
smiths: hands—pioneers and farmers
of the prairie's far firmament.

Their defeats were planted in the sky like stars,
jewels cut from the primordial ice,
                              shining…

By planting the land, they thought the land
was theirs.
              But they were wrong. Wrong
as the Indians they dispossessed, who learned
the treaties were punctuated with bullets—
and the long pauses of starvation…

They built the country that laid them in their graves.

They held the hard silence like a seed within their hearts.

And also: the night dust that consumed their lives…

II.

MOTTO

In the dark times
Will there also be singing?
Yes, there will also be singing
About the dark times.

-Bertolt Brecht

Dale Jacobson

1.

(the city asleep)

The living laid each night down
in their dreams while dust,
the tormentor,
collects on the edge of a knife…

The city is asleep—
the city has always been asleep.
Even before it was built, it was asleep
and the wind, which blew through
windows not there, was also asleep,
a somnolent wanderer—

Why is everyone so tired?

At the stroke of midnight,
the clock might skip a beat,
longing to escape outside the time,
fly backwards toward a shriveled sun,
a blackened orange that has spent eternity
devouring its own inner distance…

But something pulls the instant back
into the nativity of nurturing night:
a hurt, perhaps, long neglected,
a wounded fish on the salt flats,
some far eon that yet calls out.

Or perhaps…
only a thin voice cries out
to be saved from its petrified raft,
"The Yesterday Invincible,"
which went down years ago:

Dale Jacobson

some lone soul searching
a spirit compass in this city buried
beneath the comatic silt of stars.

Why is everyone so tired?

No government commission will ask
the dead soldiers and dead workers
who they were, broken statistically
or shot through the heart, who are
hunting the fields of the bankrupt
past—and the lights of the city
have all turned their backs,
donned formal evening shadows.

The histories of blind indifference
are yet following the river's
twilight armor into nightmare—
there on the horizon is the gleam
of the ancient armies…

Each day's murdered return
to the sea's ancient rhetorical
offices of salt—and though
the dead call out to be heard or loved,
the generals
are putting others to sleep.

2.

(American nights)

In the military night of metallic silence
drowned horses are raging in the sea.

Old men slide into their long beds
the years have stretched into longitudes,
their faces sculpted by the rain,
in their hands the law of ancestral thunder.

Two crows fly from the moon's horned diadem,
each the image of the other's departure,
towing time from the Capital of Solitude.

Luminous fences shimmer like cool bones.

In their dreams men and women whirl apart,
collide in opposing desolations. The wind
wanders the night wearing twin shoes:
one of greedy laughter, the other of generous grief.

Nostalgia longs for the wilderness of drowned clocks.

* * * * *

The statistics wilt at my fingertips:

how many Vietnamese the Pentagon killed,
how many returned dead from that far land,
always the poor, one third black, how many
death squads in South America, the Disappeared,
the Monroe Doctrine, the C.I.A., Truman's vision,
Marshall's and Acheson's... a ruinous century...

Dale Jacobson

What is it like to live in a country proposing prisons
and geared for war, dead set all ways against the poor?

Factory smoke billows into the sky,
climbs down the vertical walls: dusk horizons…

My room is often a cubicle traveling through
dead time: I wonder how we go about our work…
The street lamps glimmer in the dead of winter
while I hunt my head for words to resurrect
blazing butterflies from some sunken continent.

The news is never new: "peace broke out"—
fills my skull like a funereal bell. Television
is a tunnel that sweeps the nation into its vortex
where all prophets of God proclaim their fame—

What does this silence of brutalized blood signify,
the reposed combustion of quick-tempered sulfur,
death in the schools, fatigue of night violets falling?

The Secretary of the Department of Corpses
raises his crosier, a pale hand stuck on a shin bone.
The White House like a ship under lights sails
on the oceans of eternity into the next century.
The flags ripple across the empire…

The body a commodity on the market of the street,
the ancient lore of whoredom for the glory of gold,
pathos sold like fish hauled in from the sea…
Novus ordo seclorum: manual automata.

From the inner cities to the Eternal City of Light…
From the symbols of salvation to the dark alleys…
From the holy waters of heaven to the suffering
mortal laundry of the poor…
                                    the distances…

If I try to gather the winds together,
all those singing birds, if they come—
the guns interrupt—the enchantment
is broken—the song isn't enough—
the sky companions scatter…

The times spin us around with a sinister song.

Solipsism: like a deep fish in the cool currents,
the empty sexual hunger, net of the void
fallen through the interstices of the stars.

In the bars, men and women drink their sex away,
neutralize their terrors, sing the long day down,
stain the walls of lasting with smoking words.
They call alcohol to fill their loneliness,
a drunk or drugged wind of decay rising from
beached seaweed, the cast-off clothes of day,
while chrome insects rearrange the sea's skirt.

                        * * * * *

I look at America and shudder from the cold.

I know her victims are out there in the dusk
with ashen eyes devouring the lights.

Perhaps grief—
                    like dark bats flying through
secrecy—
                    will inherit the night sky that assigns
its lunar seal upon our sleep, retiring a nation
abandoned to bedizened bedlam.

Here we become the ghosts of ourselves,
untie our shoes, we who are weary habits,

dim shadows of children who once were bright.

I cannot proclaim the month of May, pure month,
mythical virginal month when the moon wanders
silver and clear upon the wild waters, drifts down
to the white shore and sings like the wind
to the waves in the fragrances of spring.

So many go drifting down their empty many nights
alone and cold like Orpheus singing the sun away,
down a river of wreckage and days turned sideways
where love is a familiar navy of exhausted leaves
launched toward their wintery and unswayed sea.

3.

(suicides abandon the cities)

Indeed, Bertolt, dark times these.
There are casualties who hunt out
the stones beneath rivers,
who depart without comment.

Starved for words, there are those
who don't make it, who can't bear up,
who fall deeply away, shocked by
their voices darkening, a silence
that drops like lead through their years,
who have studied without celebration
the mute cold stars more real than talk.

And if they don't starve out in the streets,
the streets starve in them, and with a fatal
precision, perhaps an eye stranger than evil,
gazing askance toward the western wind,
they walk into the only asylum left, a still place
where the fronds of ferns mourn.

Dale Jacobson

4.

(through the night)

Who did I come here to be?

"Now I lay me down"…the windows of sleep
slide upon the horizons of curved time…
Submerged beneath the dream waters, a stranger,
(perhaps yourself?)—face of a lost child,
dreams the dream of things that might have been…
                                .

O yeah, I know the shapes of extinct wolves
are gathering in the shadows of the far hills,
haunting the dusk—all they want is a drink…

They came and went duskily westward…
our ancestors—
                    whom the land ate.

All destinations return to the country
that lays us loaming, a phantom paradise
where the pillow is grave and gray.

Women walk away wrapped in a cold mist
ghostlike…
                    devoured by isolation—

Powerful America of the nocturnally lost—
Words armed to the teeth. From the armament
factories, smoke builds stairs past the trees.

> *Our father who art in the grave,*
> *Give us this day our daily dust,*
> *Forgive us our hands, as we murder others.*

Through the night the stern strum of pistons
pound out their power while molten steel
flares a flourish of sparks spun like crazed fireflies
that puncture the dark and dart into an older hour.

The wind lies upon its back heavy and drunk
with discarded newspapers—in its hollow word
the vacuous call of a conch coils into itself,
the far sound of the sea…
                              What harbor calls
dreamers under what moon round as childhood?

The lightnings of freedom like fiery thorns
are frozen in her crown,
                              Statue of Liberty,
Mother of Exiles who stares perpetually away…
"She might become the dictatress of the world;
she would no longer be ruler of her own spirit,"
John Quincy Adams warned the nation.

Churches are all locked up tight safe as sorrow
in the eyes of Mary. The factories drone
through the night a hum that mums the millennium
and makes dumb the tongue—while landlords roll
in their sleep uphill with loaded pistols like old man
Rockefeller—while in Guatemala sleep sends
children slipping sideways down the sidewalks—

Through the night the factories pound
a lull and lullaby of wilted blossoms
that fall upon all the tender ears—
the thrumming engines vibrate the skull
while sleep goes on in the undertows of hell.

And though a worker might slip, lose his footing,
foot, hand, and soul summoned into gears
more powerful than benediction, making literal

"the graveyard shift," the motion goes on—no one
hears or awakens to a silence like a body crushed…

The office buildings loom, their windows a black
luster, like sheets of water that will not cascade.

Turning upon the velocity of a fall,
in a force greater than dawn, a death
breezes past the streets!—the pools of light.
The second leaving comes when,
like a neglect falling into itself, the stranger
owned by the night is denied by day.

No second coming can come to a country
whose workers cannot come home.

An empty table by the sea gathers the dawn in.

But the furniture of the impractical world fades.

5.

(elegy in Moorhead)

He arose in his youth in the youth of morning,
into a light older than he was—his hand
unlocked the dawn. Clothed in the clothes of toil,
he stepped into the day like a waiting abyss.

If he had leapt across the arch of the sun,
from night to night like a bird, somehow
forgotten to awaken or swam coolly on
like an invisible fish through the dangerous sea!

It was his last day of labor before California called.
At 3:30 in a wide afternoon of snowy horizons,
on a black Friday 153 feet from the frozen soil,
he dropped through 18 years without a word.

John Michael Weber fell from his name,
fell like a voice leaving itself behind, a pause
in the air—a silence with no wings to open...
He fell not from grace, but to his graceless country.

His monument is a malting plant of Anheuser-Busch.
No net of hands, no rope tied him to safety.
The ravages of profit were the ravages of the sky.
At bars they drank Budweiser in the dimming dusk.

Now when the keys of the stars open the vault of night,
they shine through his absence an empty subtraction.
And the light that gathers in the halo of the moon
retires his name to the nameless prairie expanse.

Dale Jacobson

.

III.

Can't make something out of nothing…

      -working class axiom

Nil posse creari de nilo

      -Lucretius

It demands more than a belief
In our sleep
To enter the peaceable kingdom.

      -Don Gordon

Dale Jacobson

1.

(callings)

North winds nag us: and—
                        like a dance of butcher knives,
the flurry and fury of the aurora borealis.

In the advent of spring, lightning glazes the lakes,
fiery spears clash against the earth's watery shields!

Beneath it all, stillness, like an undisturbed dining cloth…

Beneath all the words of the generals, silence waits—
the void, a clean empty room…unbreakable:
the room inside the rooms of napalm in Viet Nam,
inside the rooms of prisons in America, inside
the peaceful sky the stillness remains undisturbed
after thunder collapses like a celestial empire.

From the shoulder blades of the Secretary of State
the shadow of a bird stretches out wings,
and the crow soars over the ruined village…

Far back,
in the dark behind the kitchen, yours or mine,
someone scatters the ashes from a dimming fire
and then: (in the one hour that is all the past)
roads sear across the empires!
                        The trees blaze
in the perpetual autumn of napalm: fire rain.

Somewhere at the edge of nightmare, in a vague glade
a wild shape dances, mysterious spirit singer: *the shaman*
whose vision is a fossil forest where a lone child
wanders inside a familiar terror. Lost…

Dale Jacobson

One voice alone is heavy and old as stone. We are called
to enter and awaken the forest wherein the stars
have built nests—anabasis into the unconscious continent,
another country fallen through the stars, where
thin flames flicker like quick flowers over dark lakes…

In the swirling and dangerous dark, the stranger
who knows us holds the colored pebbles, moonstruck
like a visionary city, agates the eons have washed…

Who did I come here to be? What did I come to say?

Wings of evaporation touch our lips like faint words:

> *Heirs of the year full of rivers and might,*
> *build a voice from the stillness of our voices.*
> *Build the freedoms we did not know.*
> *We went as far as we could, and then*
> *we founded our nations of sovereign dust.*
> *We dreamed once under the one and same*
> *moon, in a different time, in another place…*

2.

(litany)

The craggy citadels of the Rocky Mountains,
high jazz of the earth given shape against
the sky. No king or boss gave them time.

The Pope didn't journey the heavens,
but nailed Galileo's shadow to a crumbling rock.

No Egyptian priest or pharaoh awakened
the hand that wrested fire from its cool sleep.
The people died building the tombs of kings
in whose hearts silence like a desert reigned.

Tacitus said: "Rome creates a wasteland
and calls it peace."
                              Out of the old empires
the American empire arose—a continent arose
and then came the murder of Indians, and then
came the murder of slaves, and then came
the continued tradition of the poor while
frost convened on the margins of dawn,
on the grave stones, inscribed its cryptic gospels.

New York, Detroit, Chicago…westward—
the great cities—great pavements and architectures,
Los Angeles of Hell's Angels and pseudo demons,
the pyromaniacal white robed angels of white
man's heaven, children living on the streets,
citizens of the weather, the existential light—

Fargo, North Dakota, where Indians haunt
NP Avenue like displaced ghosts drinking
their sad history, the light of Custer's pale hair…

And further away, the countries I traveled,
with my luggage like a Pandora's package
of bitter furies, when I tried to drink my way past
my dark nostalgias, into a milder moment.

London with her black taxies like hearses
carrying the corpse of business to the funereal banks.
Madrid with her hands of poverty in Plaza de Espana.

Paris suffering from her exiled poets
while sweepers in the Tuileries Gardens
stir up the dust of the failed revolution.

Cashel and Dublin where Irish blood
still calls out to the rainy cathedral skies.

And I saw the countries my footsteps did not visit,
the blood-stained streets of San Salvador where
American liberty extends her hand like a fatal queen.

The children of Guatemala tortured in windowless cells.

When the house of Neruda was attacked, my house
fell to disorder and the walls mourned like a morgue.
Chile still trembling from the hospitality of the C.I.A.

I saw how the peasants of Nicaragua gathered
against the mercenaries paid by the White House
Drugs, Incorporated, Ronald Reagan President.

I saw the apologists arrive like scavengers
eating age, like popes of cynicism counting money,
tearing with arthritic fingers at their arthritic hearts.

I lived where no suits came around to apologize
to those who live in defunct hotels where the nights

are constructed from a conversation of creaking wood,
isolation thickening in the door knobs—where
imaginary gardens are burned down by real arsonists.

Who belongs to the condemned buildings, those children
without homes, in their eyes a sunken mote of ash?

How gentle the madonna appears in the art
portrayed among the polished stonework of
the expensive churches. But who is the *other* child
the *other* madonna cradles, black, Indian, white,
but always poor!—the child in whose eyes a sliver
of fire flies back through dark time to the first spark?

Who is the stranger we meet in sleep, child dressed
in the mantle of moon wearing our face, come to open
the doorway of storms where the forgotten histories
are constructing their silence and shadows?

> *I come with words tempered in the wars against workers.*

> *I am summoning together my bitter blood.*

> *I am rising from the darkness of moon and terror flaming.*

3.

(elementary song)

Carpenter with your wooden prudence,

bricklayer with the sea's gravity
talking through your fingertips,

farmer father of the mournful sunflower,
slender wheat, sturdy corn, secretive potato…

miner in the underground cool vaults
with eyes that see through stone,

metal smith upon whose western horizon
rust gathers to gossip through the night,

baker whose chuckle is pumpernickel
full of yeasty zest and grainy fame,

mechanic whose oil unsticks like a lyric
Newtonian physics, steel walker balancing
your shadow on air, factory worker
calling to order the wild elements,

workers, whom my country denies,
from your hands the world arrives…

4.

(what tools tell us)

My father wore a darkness under his cap,
worry cast out from his forehead
like a visor, a dead wing, as though
this might keep him hidden from
something that would not appear.

What did Norwegians ever know
but poverty and cold? And the sea.

What have the parents left us
but tools and some stories?
—the tools, hard earned, carved from winter,
and the stories quarried out of hard times.

Sometimes I feel an urgency gnawing
at the clocks, like a room I enter fatally
familiar, an anxiety at night in the floor
boards as though I can hear him pacing,
or the house were creaking like a ship...

* * * * *

I am the son of a laborer,
whose years were worn into his hands,
which had learned to obey machinery:
oil valves and gauges that required
his daily life, pipe line that fed
with dinosaur-light the engines—
and fed more money into the banks
and less into the hands of workers.

From my father I learned reverence

for the ancient oak, and the snail
in its tiny portable cave—and I learned
a *way* to listen from what he knew
and loved and worked with hands
that could feel into the habits of things:

the splintering wood that required
a delicate touch, chisels honed keen
as surgical instruments, dangerous
hammers that could wound, quick
sharp axes friend or foe, the power saw
with whose singing whirr serenity
was married like a velocity-mirror
that would throw back the undevoted blood—
tools that are the means and meaning
of the earth and punctual as lightning
writing its swift sinew across the sky.

I learned we could make the world work
only if we attended to it with patience…

One time he took me far up, with my child's
feet and heart, which knew how to celebrate
the tall days—we ascended the spiraling
stairs of the petroleum tank, like scaling
the face of a huge god. I looked down
over the city and saw from the people below
how small we were upon the immense prairie!

* * * * *

I know now what bothered him those many
years. He knew what hunger was—a fact.
The Depression of the Thirties was more
than a memory from which he had never
returned. He knew that hunger came invisibly,
like a stealthy intruder entering the clocks,

stealing everything, first eating the tools,
then the house, and at last the stories…

Once I saw the world in freedom
(only for a moment at the place he worked).
It was a glimpse, a time when I knew
my eyes were awake! I went to grab a wrench:
it glowed like a signature in the dusk!
Ancestors had left it for us, made it, given it,
molded by their hands and passed on to ours.
Then I realized how the tools are owned—
by strangers, who do not use them, nor love them.

Now I know that for a long time the tools
have been imprisoned and stolen from us,
put into bondage the same as our labor.
Our hands mourn for them like kin.
And I know that we are also enslaved,
because our hands are chained to the tools—

They are the covenant with the land,
and we must talk to the land,
or: it will eat us with silence…

It is simple:

we must free the tools to free ourselves—

what a returning destiny!

Dale Jacobson

IV

Whom to choose as builders?
Those still unborn.

Do not ask what they will be like. But
Determine it.

-Bertolt Brecht

We must walk up out of this dark
using what charms we have.

-Thomas McGrath

Dale Jacobson

1.

(by water)

All destiny is return—
                    this is law even before the sea
gave rise to the wind's hand that lifted waves,
or light flashed without warning or witness
from its crushed dark seed, condensed crystal
unsealing the void like arrows of doves.

We know the light that awakened us will turn
away: dark emptiness is opening through our bones…

There is time: for the archeologies of the earth, and:
the archeologies of burned-out ciphers,
                                        sunken stars,
the heart the vault of its own inborn stillness.

When those assaulting glaciers altered continents,
they tore the land slowly, inch by inch,
only to enter the airy strata, their work done.

    And today,
    yeah, who knows?—
    today is a bad business,
    the terrain in agony:
    history has cast us into
    its ditches, like wreckage
    where we must try
    to reassemble our collective
    memories—not under
    the pale light of nostalgia
    but out of the bones
    of the past put together
    a sextant for the future:

a time machine to bring
our own time home—

recall ourselves from fatal solitude—
word by word, in these trenches these days
these "modern" times—
                    our daily struggles…
a living…

* * * * *

But also a legacy, carved on the long wind with song,
hallowed like the moon with myth, told in the metals
of the great grandfather tools, recorded in the land,
ruins storms have eroded:
                    broken columns,
stone cathedrals with windows open to the rain's
washing catechism, their ceilings of vagrant stars…

Evidences…
          tremendous labor…

                    And beneath all
the buried foundations the sleeping daughters of
all daughters who cannot dream the dream
to awaken themselves—surrounded by fossilized
flowers:
          sleeping beauties dreaming in sleep's
nightmare in the history of sleep how each night
they rise
          under the stars to gather up the tears
of the earth,
          and hang them on the wind—
and scatter them among the dew in the grasses—
where with the thin gray of each dawn
they go on acquiring tomorrow's light.

The legacy or curse our ancestors left us
a millennium ago, or yesterday—
whose scars we inherit, under the skin.

We inherited their scars and wounded nights—
the unfinished struggle the roads remember,
we inherit distance, wind the conveyor of distance,
and all the past comes together darkly to deliver
messages: clear black lights swirling out of the night
to take us away—
                    dulled fragments, shattered relics,
the crushed throats of broken hammers, with a fury
and discipline of time, these discussions the dust
continues will not repent, cannot reduce their hours
further,
            but the past floats toward our hands nightly
like a tactile hunger. They come like shadows
to call our shadows, ancestors come to lead us down
toward cold cellars in the salty citadels of the sea…

                    * * * * *

I go to the city limits, return to the primordial
and perpetual dark, aware of the circular night
that stones contain, those anchors of time, and
the lithic gardens, flowers entombed in their fossil
tenements, and the secretive veins of swift silver!

The weathers of the dead are slow and abiding,
broken down through bone, the rain of minerals,
the dynasties buried beneath decaying constellations.

Called like the rivers by gravity, I follow the maternal
and demolishing waters that carry away in their syllables
sorrows that found no articulation among our wars.

The scriptures of lichen are silent and without prophecy,
the trees mantled in autumn forecast only winter,
but the river is a black and ancient voice—speaks
the brooding histories,
                              somniloquy of voices sinking
beneath my feet toward the sea where neither human
hand nor law prevails, the civilizations of numerical ruin
whose time is washed away by infinite drops of rain.

And so,
          I descend,
                            go to the moon's grave
where all the antiquities reside, those broken tools
nostalgic for hands that once wrote the fate of the stars,
and with my only language naked as love or light,
I call the dangerous ancient ones, the fallen workers,
whose anonymity is written in the fatality of water.

Ancient Ones loved in the salty teeth of the sea,
embraced by oblivion in your briny beds, dismissed
from your blood and your tongues, instruct me
with your absolute silence—we tear your silence
when we cut our bread: teach us our task on
these roads named terror, forgive us our obedience
to the betrayal of ourselves as we forgive others
the betrayal of their selves and between us, the world:
walk with us in your wide absences clothed in wind.

Our shadows are acquainted with your shadows.
The shadow of my hand remembers your shadow
cast outward into the centuries from the camp fire,
nearly touches that far circle of ashes.

Your eyes and mine are the same eyes—azure flames
the brackish waves devour. Give me your long, cool,
burning powers of the twilight. My shadow is married
to yours, road and liquid moon. From you I earn
my voice, this word, this hour. I am your emissary from
the disinherited dust, smashed house of muted thunder.

2.

(by fire)

Men and women and children living in the streets,
in the entry ways of store fronts in San Francisco.
Dust advances beneath an old iron glare…

The poor must make their own luck—more often than not,
not to be made. The worst of all fates: to be poor and alone,
the sifting of quicklime light through longing fingers,
empty hours like the crumbling of incendiary butterflies.
Been down so long, up looks wrong…

They come and go—not speaking of art but
changing the predators of their days, living
the unholy contradiction, law of the damned:
struggle is always social, pain always personal.

Justice without supper is not justice. We the poor
are the watchers in the dusk after the money
has been taken. The lights shimmer from
the looming office buildings. We darken.

The street forgets the irrelevant shape that smoked
a cigarette against the enormous cooling sky!
Spark lost in the…Long ago it wasn't so—
we sang when we brought in the grain. The rain falls,
slantwise, through all mortgaged dreams. Worker
returning from the factory, turning from your work,
awaiting the bus of strangers like masks of dusk,
three crows perch on the cross of the telephone pole.

They are your executioners, with eyes of charcoal.

* * * * *

The country is different from the city, but there too
words are often hollow, without roots, return fatigued…

There are places my words do not belong.
At the hills of Chankpé Opi Wakpala the wind turns
on the vowels of *another* language—words the wind lifts
like dew from the sleeping grass—in the place of much
grieving where the Wasichus massacred hundreds
of Big Foot's people, in the Moon of Popping Trees.

If land can have a voice, it rises from those who
themselves arose from its soil and though they
are murdered or dispossessed, the words
of the conqueror cannot defeat the silence
that remains: hard stone holds the crime.

The poets will speak of common ground in a land
owned—then take over the town, steal your
words and like God call it good. Someone says:
"Home is where one starts from" and then:
"the world becomes stranger." And stranger yet,
when the native voice is banished: then the world
is exile, though poets be too dishonest to say so.

I've been living beneath the age of a dying tree,
this century whose leaves have entered the next,
still asking who I came here to be, part wild animal
with one savage eye askance, testifying to these leaves
falling, my commission the office of dried laurels—
writing—
              waiting—
                          while the pages of this poem

53

shed what words they have, what color they take
from the world,
                    in the autumn of a dying empire.

In the evening the world can seem on fire,
cool, blazing, as though all change is possible!
Necessity is the leaf that falls from the tree
in which one can see the skeleton of a hand…

For many autumns the branches have lectured into the dark
while the rivers continue to forget the dirge they smash.

                    * * * * *

Could I invoke a voice from the future?—
a whisper that rises from autumn to haunt
the haunted poor,
                    a cry presiding under
our lasting darkness until we become
what the imaginary quick pen of our blood
writes upon our blank and black,
                              charred hearts—

Could I invoke a voice from the past?—all
the long dead sleeping with one hand over
the kingdom of dust—
                    I hear the trace of a voice lost
in the coming night,
                    at the edge of the wind,
                              stirring
the brittle leaves…
                    "…sabotage the ruins that own us—"
broken leaves swirling among the hollows where
the wind slides,
                    empty places where poverty speaks
with lips thinner than air…
                    and neglect can be reduced

no further and the dusk walks deeper into the darkness…

rumor of burned-out dreams—
                              could this tree
old and scarred
                give song
                            flight?—

3.

(May Day)

Our words are born from the dark choirs of the past
just as leaf, corolla and pistil shape themselves
out of the genetic scrolls wrapped within seed,
and in this calm glorified and glowing afternoon
occulted through the black territories of winter,
our language is formulating itself within our silences,
in this brown season preceding transformation
when soon the ferns will issue their fronds over the earth
like green benedictions or blessing hands, and usurp
the shriveled crosiers of their own corpses.

And out of the past, history's husk of faded and far
skies, the defeated and scattered workers must
sometime gather to unite their necessities in a time
like this one nearing May Day and meadowlark,
when soon Tom McGrath's fond bleeding hearts,
like a cartridge belt from the arsenal of buried Eden,
like messages strung upon earthen aerials,
will ride the arch of their semi-rosaries
out and over the roots of death they complete.

At:
615 Eleventh Street South, Moorhead, Minnesota,
center for ten years for my returning feet,
as the last decade has departed like dust upon
the lifeless wings of wind-blown cicadas,
when the ornamental crab tree orchestrating
its inner and idyllic order will soon accent
with a virginal constellation all its branches at once,
that same quince that seeded the clouds of all tears
and one precious tear more eloquent than all
the bourgeois poetry and "dissolute poets

who have lost Whitman's faith in the human race,"
North American literati too sophisticated to lift a fist—
in this day that extends its light upon wings of chance,
I expropriate the metaphors of the past to shatter
the past, dead season of fugitive powers.

And when the peony in its full regalia will rear up
like a pony and ride the breeze, like a danseuse
whirl in the whorls of her blooming and reign
in a stately and stalwart gown of foliage, and when
the jack-in-the-pulpit will soon peak out like a shy pope
without congregation and meditate upon the Northern
Lights in his slender vatican, a secret shade-loving amorist:
while these colorful preparations for sexual ambush begin—
still: the hell-inventing religions are stoking their fires,
the financiers in philosophical abstraction are preparing
real statistical fatalities, even as workers work toward
the work day's end—when in a reprieve almost like
freedom they relax their transmuting hands and drink
a deep draught of ancestral darkness and dawns…

* * * * *

The day is traveling, like an old man, toward
the lunar cold crown of midnight, where all beasts
bristle black with teeth shining in the swirling, eerie
wild—
         a world made for all free-ranging nightmares.

But I speak of another time when language guides us
toward our own incitations—like signal fires once built
beneath the companion immeasurable constellations.

In dawn, the descending flute of the two-noted phoebe
calls out to the possible world an enigmatic ellipsis…

The journey arrives for the child who helps invent

the journey, who awakens from the cocoon of dream,
breaking the bondage of exhausted myths,
casting off caution like the drug of sleep.

> *The moment we begin to fight for freedom,*
> *the world within ourselves is already free,*
> *the Dream has stepped out upon the long road...*

Suppose the child we all were who still lives within
each of us, who comes new to the days or wants to,
is condemned to approach the wasteland of dead
trees where the moon glazes vitrified birds.

Suppose the cereal summer remains a remote season,
the serenity of sunlight captured in the grains of wheat
shimmers cold over the fields, the horizons of hunger.

Suppose the hands of the dead continue to seek us
with their vacuous fingers from the smoke of future wars,
and widows go on opening hollow spaces in their days.

Say the bones were meant to fly upon wings of horror.

Down the early dawn streets the color of piss
the aged light walks saturated with rancor,
a presence of dusk looking for a bed among ruins.

Like Celaya, I condemn poetry that refuses
the pain of the poor, "the poetry of all who won't
take sides until the knife is at their throats"
—in the grand o'l country "poetry of witness" opera house
where the principles of the principled are proposed!

And out of the slashed throat of the pale day
a black honey settles the leaves at night, bitter
as blood, a heaviness seeping into the cellars,
and the cities drown beneath a corrosive sea.

Born out of the coffins of the moon,
a litany of silences, a regiment of dark frocks,
puts out our language with a fatal touch.

Like a husk of thunder, the mournful solemnity of a rage
left unspoken, disintegrates through our hearts.

When the value of language falls, so does the value of life:
the poor wandering the streets homeless under the stars…
or dumped into the blind graves…in countries south.

Still,
        the weaving light abides as if a singular wisdom,
and still,
                we are here, some of us, once in childhood
astonished dancers—who kept time by direct
long distance connection to the ocean's rhythms,
long discourses rising and falling those waves
rebuilding the receding frontiers of themselves.

Suppose we return to the origins, our tongue
wilts on the shore, and the immense touch I feel
rising through the sea's caverns of heavy currents,
this voice that wants to speak through us from
the mute time of sea weeds and sleep, sinks into
oblivious sediment and the stars course through
their indifferent caravans without the power of names
to call them home.

                We who do the work *are* the story.

There is no one who is not stung by the sun's
wasp of remote time—whose personal silence
is not a drum stretched over the chromosomal eons.

From our common need, the human tribe began…

Dale Jacobson

* * * * *

One day, on a day like this one of seeds and silences,
when the poor put on the face of power to cancel
power, when brigades of butterflies unseal the eyes
of the meek, when the tongue that dared say nothing
at last spits out like a curse the bitter morsel of cynicism,
futile crumbs and azyme of tyranny—when the dark
assassins will be yanked loose from their hiding,
and those words that delivered death revealed
in their archives of government secrecy, and those
who spoke them are confronted with a mirror
that cancels light by their own dark gaze, when their
fatal cipher of guns is negated by the poor who have
nothing but the names of the murdered that burn
like embers of flowers in the wide dusky fields—

THEN: beware!—

the roads that denied everything but wandering
to vagabonds whose empty pockets unthread
distance into the labyrinth of their past,
these roads our searching feet have traveled
will map the future in the cosmoramic dawn
of the skull, and like the pause before song,
will invite the walking clocks, unlock the attics
and cellars and their musty heirs—the news
shall "go among all classes of the population,"
a rumor on the wind…

and the ages come
to reside on our lips like the swift residue of light.

4.

(song out of the past)

In voices terrestrial as wheat or corn,
the vagrant migration of underground water,
buried cities of mute citizens and stone skies—
from the margins of martyrdom where
blood spelled out in unreasoning disarticulation
the distance to the sleeping strata...

> the past calls...

Poverty is a lost ring, without an eye, and America
a country lost for some time, inhabited by refugees
without refuge...

> What is it?

> No one knows—

An empty room where the moon wanes.

Dark nightly fears at war with themselves...

It is the first word spoken and respoken down
the centuries, a story of power that cannot answer
what power means while wind and water gnaw ruins...

Perhaps the desert lands, unconquerable in their arid
austerity, know something of dolphins that long ago,
in mansuetude, returned to the sea...

> the saintly wave...

* * * * *

I, born of the vestigial earth of Minnesota,
son of this land where the people walk with a fear

secretive as the moraines, saw my generation grow pale—
their internal light dim like stunted plants in a room
no one had visited for a long time…

They gave their love to the word "freedom"—
their love became disdain of other peoples.
They gave their bodies to their country's flag.
It became their pall, it became a sacred sham
while the President the Pretender saluted
the pirate flag of Enron his father saluted.

Some became doctors of aesthetics who thought
poetry could be dissected and preserved in a jar.

Others learned to speak by counting, like trained
horses. Those who ate well said heaven was just.

They refused to uncover the sepulcher where
the furies, like dusty reptile birds, brooded with
ancient bitterness.
                    Instead, steel wings freighted
with exploding pomegranates circled cities,
ground zero—whose only math was subtraction.

Meanwhile the world leaned further toward
the accustomed disorder of the vanquished millions.

And what went by way of disaster went according to
its own laws, collapsing without forgiveness, without
grace, fell in the uncaring way death talks to gravity.
In the deep territories of sleep, luminous hands
hunt midnight rivers where the moon sets sail,
voyaging to the old estuaries, parallactic country.

What trellises hung with pale roses glimmer
on the wall of the collapsing ocean wave?

Night singer,
            traveler,
                        fugitive from the rain-glazed
roads, displaced noctivagator changing your strangers,
waifs and estrays,
            wayfarers,
                        peregrinators,
                                    wind stalkers:

how much went past without you?—what word
was left unspoken so long ago it became
the rasping dryness of autumn leaves, lips
of torn paper whose message became kindling?

                        * * * * *

Sophisticated cannibalism of cold cash, cold bodies
no longer making change: war,
                        profit:
                                    golden
summer tamped into the barrel of autumn:

these paper symbols of power we spend, they
govern our lives, inside the revolving universe
energy turning—the coins fall, clink on the counter,
we know what they are:
                        who went down, sudden,
like weight,
            a caving in of the quarried light,
emptiness closing upon absolute composure.

Who was murdered, killed on the torn land—
all this time of death becomes one like grass

like water,
            like grass,
                        like sky—
                                    like grass…
                                                like money…

Again and again it happens, while the presses turn
their black ink, when the mighty ones speak,
again and again, when the mighty speak, the national
monuments remain standing but somewhere
bodies fall,
            in other countries—or in America—
the invisible poor who fight the poor—
                                    and lose.

Happens at noon or six o clock, in the habits
of each day closing, in the rising of the moon,
exiled inamorata rising over the dark sleeping
anger of our nation—who were they, who looked
as if they reached for a shining planet, a farther city
beyond the destroyed one, who were the casualties
while the flags of empire snapped in the wind?

Then the queen of the heavens released an arrow
made of light years through the heart of black time.

With what instrument do we calibrate the precision
of grief, as if the silence demands our measurement?

                        * * * * *

With eyes that are black and hidden,
crushed into the hard time of anthracite,
under the wintery lashes of hoarfrost,
I am dreaming miles beneath my personal
road,

      beneath the iron claw of the State
and the refined brutal laws of commerce,
beneath the expenses and rivers without debts
and the earth star of the prairie aster,
far beneath the seed and the corolla,
with eyes that have sunk to the elements
I am dreaming the end of war—
                           this one:
of humanity against itself—which began
the evening or era just before the stars
were named—
               and as the child I once was
could imagine clouds shaping possible beings
or new continents, I am imagining a moment
condensed in the lost eye of a lost ring
buried in the earth, like the marriage
of carbon to diamond: workers to dawn:
hard clarity that belongs to itself…
                       history
shaping a crystal recognition from all ruined days.

There is music beneath my feet, all the leaves
the seasons have held, the wings of eagles
pressed into weight, continuous rhythm unabated,
moving slowly at the speed of a coin rusting,
or the velocity of a distant language, gathering
word by word, generation by darkness, sending
its message up though our sleep, from
the shifting rock beds, the drained hearts,
the stone powers with hair of shale:
the mineral libraries putting together a vocabulary…

When night fell in the shape of many bodies, when
both culture and body became worthless, their lives
entered the silence, permanence of deep stony veins,
the dry gullies whose phantom thirst they have become.

65

Dale Jacobson

Those sunken shoulders,
                    arms,
                            hands the world let go,
eyes the light let go,
                    mouths that went unheard,
having arrived at the end of distance,
                                    they went as far
as memory travels…
                    left only the odd hollowness
of time:
        the skeleton of a bird on a thorn branch:

    voices out of the wind, out of the ditches,
    voices in the green leaves opening the air,
    drawn up in the water pillar of the popple,
    voices that have forgotten their own names,
    whose legend we are, children of the dead—

    voices that flew south, or leaned into winter,
    were taken away, betrayed by the war,
    fell into the dark at the edge of talk,
    voices scattered with no place to go,
    became rumor, became lost, became ourselves…

    It isn't the lightning that frightens us,
    not thunder, but the pause that might
    swallow up our long mysterious question—
    as others have gone before who gesture
    like the leaves in autumn gliding down,
    like words that did not connect in life—

From beyond the branch where the moon sinks,
from the dark at the edge of the tilth,
                                    returns
the mourning dove…
                    far messenger…

out of the diaphanous dawn reposed against
all the sleeping daughters and sons…
                                   lost voice…
lifted from the nest of the wind a still place…
                                        broken
world…
            calling out from its own white silence,
with the cold like solitude draped upon wings…

    —does not speak to our bitter rituals,
    not the battle where three walls
    of the house fell, nor the mercenary
    who wiped from his hand the worker's
    blood onto the leaf of the tree,
    nor the dog transported upon fire
    in a crazed whine of animal smoke,
    nor the worshippers awaiting
    incense, nor even the great requiem
    the rhythms of the ocean…

Does not speak to these things…

The legacy of struggle that brought us here remains
ourselves…

        The earth speaks to us—
                            our tools
talk to us, our sleep talks to us, though we forget
how the dark energies of the earth dream who we are—

It is heavy. Our hands become heavy, the weight
of fate unchanged, words unspoken or said alone.

How many centuries has shimmering noon waited?

The communal voices of the dead
                            rise up in our throats:

inhabit the stillness beneath our words, inhabit our words,
cry of the universe,
                    all the long call of the past—

Cities of phantoms…
                    cities of fantasy…
                                        cities
of our sleep and dream…
                    I invoke you…
                                        like light…
like shadow…
                    like ancient fire…

PART II

The rain
Never falls upwards.
When the wound
Stops hurting
What hurts is
The scar.

-Bertolt Brecht

We carry all the news with us.

-Meridel LeSueur

Dale Jacobson

I.

I don't build a house without predicting
the end of the present social order.

-Frank Lloyd Wright

Dale Jacobson

1.

(fire and voice)

Far fires of the fugitive past, vacant in the round hour
of ashes,
            lost hours,
                        ashes scattered in ancestral memory…
The long legacy of labor sung on the rumoring winds…
roads fallen into earth…
                        cities…
                                    monuments…

Our brooding history: fatigued and elongated shadows,
dark partisans of the dust,
                        usher in each nightfall…

    (The engendering roots allowed all possibilities—
    I remember when the days were more promise
    than endurance—long ago, or seems so, before
    the dangerous place names and people,
    before the displaced people with their names,
    when I came hunting joy upon the ancient earth
    and loam released a power of sleeping hours
    in the dance and glow of the moon-lit leaves…)

Ancestors transported fire their own legend
under stars when no compass measured directions—
they left solstice temples of dolmens and oghams—
journeyed as the stars journeyed, carried fire
inside the Great Night of the Blind Wandering.

    (Once upon a time in childhood the sway
    of breeze in tall branches called me,
    and wind wended my way haunting my ear
    with low words through the weeds—

along the ditches—where the high-slashing
grass murmured an old story of passing—)

Into the far night our distance goes on perishing
and yesterday's dust touches theirs, those ancestors—
and the cities burn, lamps pushing away the darkness—
like the ancient fires, our inherited light…

(Later, growing past childhood, I learned
how the trees spoke in the wind
with the past held in their water-fed rings,
the wind soughed a sound of sirens
and sailors and shattered oars given over
to the hollow-craddling waves of the sea,
and vagabonds on all the skid row streets
were the children of a cold citizenship,
lost reply in cities of desolate footfall…)

The cities put on colder faces, and beyond those
lamps,
        out past the city limits, the nights enormous
and wide
            the swirling remote colonies of stars—
the moon a pale naked celestial rose, stars like thorns,
wild sidereal garden,
                    ancient,
                            indifferent…

While the mighty engines turn,
                        and the dynamos purr
like demons feeding the gargoyle lamps of the labyrinthine
streets, our cars take us neither closer to nor farther from
home, beneath the high stone buildings with shadows cool
as slate—
        and ourselves
                    near always to the past like distance
to the stars,

      nightly there but far—and each day returns us
to the wordless wind lengthening upon something like
loss—
      what happened?—
             who never spoke?—
                    words
no one heard—
      a world that never arrived...

    (Later, looking for work, I wandered the city
    under the dome and ecclesiastical cold
    of St. Paul, where poets were busy building
    horizontal scaffolds to enter a lofty hole
    in the sky across the river, where they thought
    a personal heaven of fame could be made).

No ledger can record all those hours, dry angers
like a thirst for yesterday's rain, the faces of people
intense returning from work, the fires of dusk
laving their features, with endurance frozen
in their looks, locked like basalt inside their eyes...

    (I saw the rivers of light in the city,
    cars streaming down the freeways,
    rounding the turnpikes like swirling energy
    out of primordial release: like the photons
    of a star weaving, hunting a center—
    the city a solitary blazing flower on the dark
    prairie: commune of the lost—
                    restless,
searching,
      everyone hungry to be known...)

2.

(water and dream)

Water meandering the geological cellars…
                                        Submerged
inscription of hollow time signatures worn into rock…

Subterranean rivers flowing beneath all seasons
in their dark pure cold beneath clay pan ceilings
in soporific motion in the sedimentary house…

Aquifers we dream toward when evenfall levels
the hierarchical light, recessive voices in the chasmal vaults—

—And so we descend with the water, our beds like rafts
carry us upon meditational currents, undertow
of spent time,
                exhausted hours.
                                Dreaming we voyage—
upon waters that absorb all defeated images…

The walls of inward space open the distance
like the four petals of a phantasmagorical flower,
like an inversion where the past presents the drama
of its needs, gives shape to its discontents—its sullen
complaints—and we journey back through our own
private troubles and terrors until we are taken
by a darker and deeper momentum into the night
of humankind—
                toward the hour of origins.

This is no usual provincial American wish trip—we've
departed the national borders. This is a scan across the span
of the chromosomal zodiac of our common universe.

Toward the most remote dawn the moment is turned.
The moon of mysteries, wrapped in its young light,
like a ghostly night-ranger, descends the earliest horizon.

The waters phreatic ripple out of the stone archives,
cleansed of our history, in the *somewhen* before the stories
were spoken, in the pre-alphic age.

                We slip back further—
beyond the beginning of the planet itself, past the ignition
of fusion in the sun, riding the solar winds in reverse,
the unmaking of the galaxy, and return to the *primum mobile,*
implosion into zero hour, the house of absolute reduction!

The universe shrinks into its own eternities, collapsing
into itself until singularity unifies everything in an all
points contradiction—the instant when everything began!—
and blasts and blazes in a protean burst the original
omnihorama of genesis!—(which no one saw)—city
of all cities!—
           factory of all factories!—creation of
the dimensions that govern us, the dialectics of opposition:
change:
        the strange wobble and ripple of space and time!

Yes, we are definitely out of Kansas, past the corner drug
store, and the "stars and stripes" are a different meaning
here!
     Ad astra per aspera—all to come, all the difficulties…

In the mega-light-surge of the dilating moment
(across what expanse and time?)—the whirling
millenary masses locate a center of gravity, (while we,
dreamers not yet dreamed, linger in limbo like spacial
negatives…), and the planet Gaea forms, the Earth
we would like to call home, place unnamed drifting
within a larger place unnamed, its tectonic plates shifting

in the geological quiet—and then!—

                             the stormy void
moves,

       the earth orders its predilections for the Possible.

                                  * * * * *

And out of this scope of time is revealed to our psyche
in the past a vision, idea, image, or feeling—our ancestors
saw to the limits of their light and villages sprang
out of sea foam, out of quantum foam where each word
contains its opposite: each particle that sustains the world
reflects its satirical twin in its birth—as the regressive
hall of mirrors shatters and reshapes all images and
from this holographic kaleidoscope our world is born!

Ancestors built what they could, from what chance
provided them to build with—and now our vision
is revealed to us as it once was to them, as we return
from our return to the beginnings:

                            vision, light, need
that belongs to us all:

                    cities of shifting shape,
glowing and charged structures,

                         hypnotic architectures
floating on misty wings wafting,

                      in eerie light…
vague monoliths like the Stonehenge drifting on air—
or cities like sails, vast Clipper ships that take us
into ourselves,

              still uninvented and if only for a glimpse
released—

          the imagined cities:

                   in the communal future
somewhere awaiting builders:

                 vaporous…

diaphanous…

hazy…

fantasy levitated:

cities free as our dreams

built from what elements,

born from what beginnings?—

* * * * *

Would it be possible we free ourselves, who are still
caught

in our negative past and purgatorial houses,
in our wearied cities…

the homeless—and the half dead
slaves who don't know better,

who don't believe better,
who wear a driven lost bored terrible emptied, not even
terrified look, in this lost nightmare—real?

We've seen the cities disintegrate—from fire bombs,
from neglect,

from power—Robert Moses who freed
no one.

Many hands make the city—many voices—
the city one life shifting its shape—trying to be born
into something unknown where the wind also is a citizen—
like Goldfield, Nevada, when the I.W.W. workers
ushered into noon the commune—for an instant made
the streets free—before the Governor resurrected
the cold guns and iron armies of the bedding sea…

Often enough we performed the rites of passage,
carried the stones,

the bricks, and built the cities up,
carried the joists and plywood on our shoulders, endured
sun or winter winds,

endured harsh words, the bossing of

79

bosses who knew less than we,
                         trusted in God as though
God could be bribed, trusted in money we never saw,
in country though many were homeless, believed
national borders as if the winds obeyed them, believed
in the flag as if it were magic as if the wind could be
conscripted, believed in banks as if they were sacred,
believed all sanguine words to save us but our own—
and never won the right to pass into our own cities—

The dark gates did not shift—
                         in the illusory moonlit mist…

Cities drifting desolate in forbidden time, empty
and locked out beyond touch, in a future locked from
a nation that locks out and locks up the poor, 3% in jail—
the vision will not open except we enter together
those cities that fade into their dissolving waters,
a liquid mirror vanishing as we return to our country,
caught in our time when the alarm shakes us out
of the cocoon and womb of the universal union—

Then,
      in the moment our dazed eyes widen
to heavier light than dream, our harsh and rented day:
our physical rising:
                  toward work:
                              toward
these poorer cities we've built but never ruled—
then,
      we enter the reality where our imagination
is put to sleep,
                  governed by images we do not govern,
by violent discontent,
                  poverty,
                              anger—the past
put to sleep,

        governed by propaganda from those
who govern us in these cities not ours,
                      which we
cannot praise,
         but endure…
               sustain…
                    bear…
abide,
      even when our eyes against them close…

3.

(my testimony)

Going to and from school in Marshall,
in the Minnesota of my long childhood silence,
solitary walks were freedoms—reprieves
or escapes—when I listened with crystal ear
to the old magics, voices I somehow
recognized, squirrel chatter, bird chirp,
though their language was beyond words.

And I felt the order of things complete
when blackbirds conspired to kidnap
the wind—and sparrows, like small
punctuations practiced impatience.

And once as only once is arrival, then
I studied the earth, not for names but for
her habits: how the gnarled oak,
the twisted strong wood sinew, its great roots,
derived deep from the mother mysteries,
and the long blasting winter winds,
tumbling down the northern hollows
with the low wail of deceased Blues Singers,
crusted the snow in the open fields
to crunch solid beneath our heavy boots.

And March or April came with the waters,
glistening rivulets in the light of the thaw,
and along the sidewalks the branches dashed
bright islands among their shadows—
and the air itself seemed to shine.

> *From my own name outward I went,*
> *listening for the foreign names*

that were passports into the world,
seeking to make the strange familiar—

seeking the communal speech
from dawn to dusk—from
balmy May to melancholy October,
the seasons the moon sojourned.

Came the wind from the far waters,
and the night-signing lightning born
from its black floating mountains,
and the cooling rains—

I learned the earthly elements, the dark
nitrogens in the soul of their soil,
the composite granite, and the metals
that made my father's tools hold an edge.

All wide and wild forces multiplied
the language of my town—and the prairie
of corn stretched out into the night
where the dew and star wed...

* * * * *

And who was I then in the large room the world
except animal yearning to become human,
hunger of body and silent hunger of word,
spell-bound in dream realm, a youngster
in an unknown world: learning to lose…

…in that school, where the hallways held
a smell so ancient it had become
its own secret—and the wood floors
creaked of dust glued together by wax.

An old ship listing into the prairie,

there I heard the whines and rattling
in the water pipes rhyming like trapped
time rising from the basement where
workmen descended so far back into
subterranean passageways, I imagined
hollow-eyed skeletons staring at dead
light bulbs like a lineage of caretakers,
those burned-out lights like the lost years.

Hollow eyes enduring, a long descent
of ancestors I saw, empty eyes from below
whose hunger had grown so cunning it had
disappeared…become the spaces through which
night hawks spoke, had become one with the dusk
when my own eyes dilated…eyes of the past
Blake knew brooding over the nations.

Those iron pipes clanked out signals, water pipes
haunted by the dead, spoke a code of geological
discontent, and they caught and captured my wild
and water-born instincts with rhythms of far time,
whose grammar I couldn't learn: to be alone…
among the powerful dead!—(the angers of history
I didn't then know but felt, a solitary inheritance)—
alone like a Norwegian troll called to the caverns,
underground energies stored in archeological
archives, in the silence beneath the geoide,
in the realm of stalagmite cities, mineralized
hours, obdurate endurance of stone which not
all the human anguish of history could cause
to crack, to swallow up one tyrant.

* * * * *

At fourteen I wasn't to be found.

Scattered…

torn apart by the hungry contradictions…

I walked my home town as if whole, but with my head
low—
       weary.

          I was at war with myself like my nation.

I was already haunting like an orphan my own ground—
common to no one—where I had never found
what I yearned for: the freedom to play—while
my parents replayed the old fights of my grandparents.

The time of play had ended.
There was no time for play.
I knew it as I knew the roads that led nowhere were all far.
I was scattered over the landscape of my own land
like someone fallen apart a little at a time, but kept going on…

Pieces called to one another,
                     each without a language:
a foot riding the winds of the glaciated sky, searching
like a lost nostalgia for a familiar road home—an eye
somehow planted on the dark side of the moon,
in infinite midnight scanning the void for the face of God—
a hand perpetually delivering the local newspaper,
The Independent that never reported any independent
news, while the war went unreported, the massacre of
the Vietnamese, while the river continued its way toward
the estuaries widening into the sea—millenary wash.

From the old iron bridge on Fourth Street I watched
the Redwood River, the water combing the green hair
of the stones,
           moments that were reprieves or escapes,
the free waters insistent upon descent as I stood there
wondering what had happened—

85

                                                   why the ordinary
was strange and I a stranger haunting my own soil
like a melancholy mournful ghost of my own life,
attracted to deeper, and deadlier, underground rivers.

Surviving was difficult as an Osiris among
the scattered images,
                           dispossessed world:

I was too young to be a cosmology.

If not the psychic body, the physical one must be whole,
must coordinate the parts—learn to act as tomorrow
requires though the mind says yesterday is still wrong.

And those patriarchs of that public school
(where all pain was private), righteous
in their liturgies of the national palaver, ordained
the sacred rights of the rich while the poor
were duty bound to die for the rights of the rich.

They imposed a cold order, a clamorous clinquant
indoctrination,
                      a jovial jingoism where intellect became
catechism…
                      and love without a word to rhyme
(or put on the wings of a dove to climb the sky)
shrank to cynicism! It was a program to deny feeling
(like good bland prosaic minimalist or "language" poets)
and the low counties of despair where I lived had no vote
in the body politic—no say no song along the way…

They said: cut-throat competition brought out
the best in people. They said: business is business
and the business of America is business (Calvin Coolidge).
They said: what is good for General Motors is good
for America (Charlie Wilson). They said: patriotism

is sacrifice (sentiment the rich have sense to avoid).

War became peace; profit the national good;
the Russians bad (very bad) and aliens unknown
from outer space were already the enemy—
paranoia of the universe and the future, anything
beyond the borders of the national mirror, was sanity.

And all those veterans who had fought in what must
have been the eternal closing of spring, World War II,
cheered the war against Viet Nam—they had learned
so much from all that death—their love become a flag.

These were the lessons my teachers taught and those
lying bastards that shat on my head (concerned of
my hair-cut first) paid no notice to the elastic boy
stretched across a land of contradictions,
                                        trying to pull
myself together…
                    the suicidal parts…
                                        —even as I
believed them and wrote Platonic thoughts against Marx
to defend the Republic (of Plato?) for history class where
no class struggle existed, I wondered what had happened,
wondered where I had gone wrong,
                                or my hand, or foot,
or head—
            which part had confused the others—
                                                even as
the people,
            the poor ones suffered even as my own living
was heavy and hard, living beyond the summers of the long
and dead dreams:

            blue cities in ruin upon the ionic
            and acrid plains on the other side
            of lost lightning that once brought forth

Dale Jacobson

the young and mythic morning where
all brightly-colored birds sang...

                                          gone,
difficult to let go—
                    the time...
                               to leave behind the whole
world for the emptiness and loss—
                                  a nation where
only money talked and those without were mute,
my hand enslaved to *The Independent,* the town
newspaper that perpetuated the great lie of
the great poet but stupid patriot Horace:
Dulce et decorum est pro patria mori (while the bodies
kept coming back from the war in disposable bags)—
no one quoting H. L. Mencken, that sardonic witness
long before the poetry of witness became noble:
"Whenever you hear a man speak of his love for
his country, it is a sign that he expects to be paid for it"—
no one asking who got paid for all that death...

my hand that *needed* a hand become a device
of the newspaper whose news was the propaganda
of my nation whose power took from the poor
to give to the rich even as I learned incentive—
learned the psychic mechanism for bribing the soul—
to work not for love but private wealth—to be selfish—
to earn a future mummified with money while all
electrical signals deep in my cells said:

                              "incite to sing!"

And so:
        for the perpetual future of private wealth,
small country of the American Dream outnumbered
by the collective poor,
                        I learned to dismiss the incitation

88

of body and spirit,
                    the one and only human spark kindled
for the purpose of exchanges of light,
                              the need to come
to others—
            to belong—
                        arrive—toward love, burning
like deep-sea lamps long ago risen to the cities,
like the streetlights that gathered their circling
frenzy of moths,
                    winged notes of the moon
                                        whose
message is dance,
                    gyrating in time lag,
                                    when
my father and brother and sister planted trees in early
autumn
            far into dusk loamy—
                              working in the center
of human silence where words sounded the size of a house,
the shared solitude,
                        communal,
                              I knew—
                                    inside
the distance, the universe whirling, the social galaxy
rushing through the void:
                        the work a joy a connection
to the dark
            watchful
                        ancestors I imagined in the night,
as labor become legacy like wind entered my muscles...
free...

        Now a far memory turning...
                              shrinking
    like a small theater curving eastward
    under the moon:

a small time…
whose voices,
            still speaking there,
here come to stillness…gone where
the world calls nothing back, but keeps
turning itself
            in its greater drama of countries
that resemble our ruined journeys—
…even now,
            as I would incite to song
all the praises we would have made
and are still
            unsung…
                  stillness stilled…
in this coming darkness I recognize by danger!

II.

Four Faces

Dale Jacobson

1.

(childhood)

…begins with water,
                            its arriving narratives sloping
toward roots,
                    the play of light in the time of play and days
ablaze as I sometimes still see them in the vision and vigil
of a younger eye,
                        in a strange calm,
                                            remembering…

how I walked the river with my brother,
                                            walked
the countryside,
                    and the rainy musk of moldering spring,
sweet grasses,
                        swirled up with wet fragrances cool
as the jay's heraldic cry was sharp, when I rose
a wanderer to my own country in the open day,
and drifting fields of the prairie knew my feet
and I studied the river,
                            stones whose green hair
the waters combed, the corn leaping from
deep loam toward the early mornings of June.

My story and ours is told in the laws of the struggle
against the fall of time,
                            the slant of light in evening,
the calling elements that spoke age, iron's anger
the smokeless fire of rust eating the tools, fatality told
in night's powerful family,
                                the eyes of ancestors
near and distant as the stars and hard as flint!

Against the fall of time…

my story and ours…
I found
my reflection in the drowning depths of the dark waters
where the moon whitely glistens:
how we came…
once—
from following the rivers,
fishing the communal
suppers,
from the river that rules by long descent
they lived, wandering the shores of the waters where
the graceful body wove like a fluid shadow,
vitreous fin,
shape of sleek obsidian,
wounded and driven down
by the swift spear that crashes all flowing senses!—
life into food!—
life's sacrifice feeding life!—
and they
lifted bloody the heavy husk shattered beneath its own
naked sheen,
gasping and torn,
broken image on broken
water,
the twisting imperative of death.

They cast up the soul of the fish into the starry heavens…

And with this death, from the sky's inversion, the birth
of our migration…
the history of rivers began,
while the sunken beds like the unconscious mind
slept beneath dark and mysterious currents where
silence went on spawning its dream of life.

Blood on the waters!
Later: blood on the roads…

The rest is history. And later: the American Dream where
the poor lived in the wealth of a future that never arrived.

Still, in the indivisible stillness of all time, once the tribe
was one,
          clear in common need,
                    primitive necessity,
called to survive,
            summoned by the rivers to follow
an unknown future—as were my brother and I—
ignorant how the future was already ambushed
and two million Vietnamese would die from corporate
bullets made to wobble to do the most damage,
the M-16, or from shrapnel of spinning "lazy dog"
bombs, brutal—or from napalm—
                    ignorant as we stole
our fish (and freedom) from the nearest river, in days
when we couldn't imagine the cities whose foundations
were lifted skyward—
            cities falling as Truman's
"rain of ruin"—
           or Johnson's—or Nixon's—or the Bushes'
fascination with fire—
            anarchical architects of the empire—
building chaos: rearranging the bones of the poor!

And so we studied light's play upon the water as we fished
bullheads, tough leathery beasts of the deep we yanked
from the mud—ugly hook eaters,
                survivors:
their grandfather faces thorny,
             primitive,
                familiar—
the eyes and mouth of dark instinct we somehow knew—
and the death that glazed those eyes my body
recognized coldly like it knew hunger was an older

story that had a physical history beyond myself.

I learned that words made up the power and possibility
of the world—ranging far beyond the dumb mud where
the bullheads idled and wallowed:
                                    words that made
each life its own myth shared with all others—all myths
part of one so immense,
                            inside the one stillness,
that no one could write or speak it all.

But words were tied to hunger, hunger to its legacy,
the roads that brought the rhetoricians with their
catechisms of chrysological mythomania by which
the poor always died: poverty—oppression:
words no one should say in the USA of denial—

And yet,
as all were once children, we were all outside
the rule of the State—
                        for a young time in a world
that seemed ours: our language free, the corn not owned,
and our brothers not yet dead in war—
                                        not yet
casualties of this home of dying, those cities of serious stone,
the cemeteries inside the one stillness, this fossilized light
of a brooding land where people speak alone, where time
is alone,
            victims always alone, as I came to know
migrating through my years:
                            Armies of the Dead
and the Living Poor always anonymous as I went
hunting my own name, as I migrated through my years
like my ancestors once followed the rivers,
                                            guided by
water to the seas of their exile and guided by their own
hearts of lunar logic to survive on something like

water's music…
                    listening…
                              to time's fall…
down the long and longing roads blind travelers invent.

Always they yearned toward something like freedom
when the hours of the earth could be released from its own
heavy fatigues,
                    or from their autumnal and camouflaged
poverties made in the colors of decaying green, like
a soldier's uniform—green as grass going brown toward
autumn—
                    colors for which the bright flag of the nation
never flew except in their deaths, silence more obstinate
than skin of stone: so much presidential promise while
the dead leapt out of their skeletons into the net of the stars…

I came to the night of terrors,
                              the sky ancient with
centuries suffering,
                         I came to the night of the defeated
distances,
                    distance emptied into distance—
                                        I came to
the Sleep of the Grotesque more grotesque than any
bullhead we ever caught, Presidential scam-artists whose
craft is chaos,
                    real body parts scattered over the ground,
psyche or soul shot out of its ruined house to go where?

I saw the images gone into the night—and
the Dancer of the Rains arrived who communes with
the Lost—arrived like mist over the graves to reassemble
the formal ceremonies,
                         the fatal happenings, the syllables
whose teeth are still gnawing the dust, to speak again
the hollow cry out of the valleys,

mournful: they
were all there!—
my mothers and fathers,
family
of strangers but known,
called up in mythical aura,
calling their own son in the world from which they
were disinherited,
calling by shimmer and shine of fluid
moon upon the dark waters…
the rippling rhythms…

Water…

Dream…

Myth…

rivers by which the tribal commune camped (I see them
gathered on the ocean floor round a dim memory of fire—
lamenting Hiroshima)
and my eye like an orb smoking
and searching,
caught between two worlds,
The Past and The Future,
descended into
that internal stored light, Dream or Nightmare
or the Reality beyond real estate,
descended amazed
and attracted by the gravities,
elusive shadows…

I returned to the Sunken Keep of the Quiet Voices,
beds dark and mysterious, where I gathered their hopes
for my own,
the People of the Water,
whom we still are,

and their seasons,
>   *which are also ours,*
>   I gathered up—
in that apparitional theater where the unsettled ruined
history,
>   from the original sacrifice of a fish onward,
became a legend
>   like a wound,
>   a scar,
an inheritance,
>   weapon of my communal senses.

2.

(initiation into work)

Seemed an old knowledge of the adults,
                              a ritual
whose meaning came from the elements, born
from the earth's rhythms, or declared by the chatter
of the chanting sparrows in the cool gray dawn
when the foreman unlocked the door of this
dominion of machines where our steps
on the factory floor sounded enormous against
the opaque quiet—
                    our voices those of intruders
entering the cool precise silence of steel, machines
in their metallic trance like hibernating beasts
in the condensed dark of their grease and gears,
the intense windings of their motors. And beyond
the strict codes of currents that moved their joints
into life, it seemed something inhabited their depths
more dangerous than physics: an atavistic memory
of once-hunted animals whose cries chilled the night!

And when they groaned it was from the depths of an abyss,
from the center of the earth's slumber—where the past
remains unannihilated—and they awoke reluctantly,
sluggishly, gathering up the strengths from the store
of night, from remote powers that had begun the world,
the strength of earlier labors, all workers whose hands
had pulled history forward to another dawning,
the steel murmur and rhythms those machines spoke…

I came there to that place of struggle full of dread and terror,
sensing separation from my young skies (where my anger
like a fierce hawk with blazing eyes already circled)—sensing
a fugitive sadness like a ghost guiding me deeper into

myself,

an instinct of my blood where I felt solitude
was heavy as the oppressions absorbed by the earth.

I came to the adult weariness of workers, the language
of curses, though I did not curse, but raged secretly
without words, like a dumb animal that only felt.

Told my country was free, I felt far from it—just as
the fruit juice we concocted there was far from Eden,
and the machine I was supposed to tame, the bottle
washer, screamed and steamed through its maw
like a sea dragon whose wrath moiled in its guts.

The monotonous and whirring motors siphoned
the eternal energies—took what was fed them,
and pumped the condensed sweetness into bottles
marked for profits—which we never saw.

The sky-planted citadels extracted that sweetness…

I remember vaguely wondering once, surprised at
my irreverence: if Marx was wrong that wealth comes
from labor, why do the rich grab workers' wealth?
And later surprised that Lincoln agreed with Marx.
Such thoughts a high school student shouldn't have!

For this glass of juice, this succulent time of fruit,
this communal drink whose fragrance and flavor
is the distance of rain gathering, for this glass where
the time of our labor is joined, distilled down
to a pure agreement among our physical efforts,
this glass we fill together from dawn to dusk
with our dark internal blazings—

our energies
we summon up from destroyed sunken continents
of the wasted summers—

for this glass of sunset
we have made together,
for this essence of earth
which is also the essence of our labor—for the value
of our labor transformed into money, for this money
from this fruit that came from the enchantment of
the sun's drop in the flower's nectar,
we worked
and were paid minimum wage,
but there was no love
to our labor: what we made was owned, the machines
were owned, and our love our light our labor
was hauled away in the dry accounts of the wind.

* * * * *

An academic asks me: "Who are all these workers
in your poem?"
Perhaps a prerequisite to a doctorate
is the surrender of sentience…Or too often seems so.
My question is: who are all these academics?

The intelligentsia with its bankrupt intellect, its false
gold of fools,
floats away on self-levitating podiums
mumbling of classical isles without class histories, all
history the anomaly of a moral norm only they know,
those talking heads impervious even to a loose
pogamoggan. Plato was right to suspect the rhetoricians,
though he named the wrong ones: people who think
in six syllables can't count to two…
And two,
as we know, is an important number—
light/dark:
work/rest:
moon/field:
man/woman:

one could say
the world is created from the number two. One doesn't go
far alone—
a road that ends in the horizon, a vanishing point.

All education begins by counting to two.
And zero is
an education that ends fast!—nothing in the cupboard
can make the emptiness in the sky greater than
all the numbers of stars! It is a fact also that people
need to eat—the homeless who are the true minimalists,
whom the minimalist poets haven't noticed.
And the child
also needs a future worth growing into—in whose eyes
the old world comes new—where the water-transferred
dreams take shape:
it took the belief of a child to hurl
the fish into the attic of our mythical house, to cast it up
from the underwater darkness, from the time-demolishing
rivers,
into the eternal Order of Pisces.

But it was the huge scarred hands of workers that opened
the world, and brought home the starry legends.

* * * * *

You risen from the lethargic impulse of the earth…
risen from layers of red iron and stone clenched together,
workers called by thunder's reverberating avalanche
to climb the ladder of metals, your tools spoke to the earth—
it understood your language, its winds rumored the long
journey toward the cities that float upon the dawn.

The Many Who in the brain of intelligentsia, the invisible
unpropertied workers whose names have no place
in the records of real estate, you to whom no Casa Real

103

belongs—anonymous workers who gathered the stones
to build the cities, who changed the manner of rivers,
who tamped the roads, tilled the fields: yours is the blood
never real to history—
                    it fell onto the land,
                                    your bodies
fell into your countries,
                        your lives fell and no voice spoke,
the stillness spoke no number but remained the silence
of zero,
        the stillness took you and no famous words said:

    this was the place you walked,
    this was the land you knew and worked,
    this was the place you mined iron,
    this was the place you quarried the stone,
    this was the place you brought up the coal,
    this was the place you leveled fields,
    this was the place, and through your hands
    the wheat passed, through your hands
    the centuries passed, and the harvest moon
glowing
        took small steps down the rapids of the rivers,
the flour came pure and the bread was passed to other
hands,
        and the money was passed to other hands—
all came from your hands—the money that rules
the stock market,
                    from the calendars chipped in stone
to the time-wandering mathematics stored in the data
granaries of computer chips like finite solar systems,
the flexible and rigid plastics, twentieth century clay—
all came from your hands, this is the beginning—
your hands raised the day whole as people are bound
together inside the one stillness, as the woven rope
tightens its sinew and suspends gravity, as the lumber
with its fibrous solidity and sturdy resonance supports

the house, the conjunctive bricks and the binding mortar,
all by your hands joined,
                              hold together the foundation
and the wall, as we are joined to each other—as
water is joined to water and love to love,
                                        and also
the matrix of the ores,
                         married to fire, the metals reborn
in the foundries in their liquid skin blazing out of smoke,
shimmering,
              capturing the light, the far origins in the sun—

Farmer whose seeds swelled from the rain's cool intimacy,
weaver whose threads translated the sea's tide
in the rhythmic loom,
                         artisan who captured fire in glazed
velocity on the clay cup,
                            assembly worker whose caravan
of cars transported the century,
                                 steel walker who bolted
together the windy seams among the gliding wings:
workers who work the elements: you understood
the sensible necessity that binds people, among
all hands equally: the unrelenting
                              inevitability:
all things are full of labor—
                         while behind your forehead,
like blue horizons,
                  freedom vaulted!

3.

(fire and voice)

Through our hands it all passed,
                              the elements we brought
together that talked to each other through our tools.

And also the world we lost or failed to invent passed
through our hands.
                    Or was taken from us: for
the profits of the wars, as Eisenhower warned:
(at Rocky Flats…where they manufactured the end
of the world: the elements whose quantum ferocities
of the sun's sudden blazing distances once took up
residence in the cities of Hiroshima, Nagasaki and left
only shadows of people on the walls, and illuminated
for an instant of cracked time the ghostly scalps of Indians
among willows weeping over the rivers, where
all the poor kneel in the mournful American Dream).

Whose rimy arithmetics leave workers in the cold homeless?
Who calculates percentage of profit as a factor of wind chill
even as stones keep their habit of containing silence?

With a look of hysterical boredom, a gaze of distraction,
or the eyes of a shark rolling inward when it strikes,
who spoke for the world, who is Ronald Reagan,
"the great communicator," founding father of the Contras,
who are "the moral equivalent of our founding fathers,"
who is George Bush the C.I.A.'s father of the Drug Dealers,
who are the fathers of the U.S. Exodus Corporation,
or Kennedy Johnson Nixon Bush of the Perpetual War?

This is the voice, language of ledgers of profit and loss
lost world forgotten long Trail of Tears that kept on

traveling across the nation into the twentieth century
and further into the center of the cities the haunting tribes
migrating toward Hoovervilles, Reagan Ranches, Bush's
thousand points of light camp fires inside the sequestral
looming dark the ragged homeless who gather in the alleys
down by the rivers beneath the bridges the ancient tribes…

—while the voice of the one who is asleep and refuses
to awaken speaks, whose mechanical eye of a satellite
or executioner translates all far signals into a private
dream of U.S. pilots dropping napalm on Guatemala
and Viet Nam, the pure idea of empire blazing,
the voice of power whose hand rules by nightmare
flames, by death squads, whose nation is the Disappeared
founded by the C.I.A. corporation, its goons poised
for assassination in venomous servility—who drops
the bodies by dim dawn into steaming volcanoes,
alive the voices falling into the earth, breathing
the altitudes of sky falling, the helicopters hovering
above the falling bodies in glistening cool logic
the mechanic rhythms of whirling steel whipping
down the air like great metallic insects powered by
tremendous combustion: over the estates of poverty—

the President's hand moves by the light of burning bodies.

4.

(commune)

So much power and so much poverty!

The jets descend the roaring groove of their own winds…
but another wind stirs the gloomy quietudes—no voice
to those lives torn out of themselves,
                                    discarded casualties
become history,
                    and the generals who trade in bodies
can't conquer these dark solitudes collecting inside
the dusk dew, in the naked grasses where grasshoppers
grind charcoal knives,
                        honing the eternities,
                                                those
lost or those that will be:
                            condensations of time
in those tiny droplets clinging to the green blades,
light years of stars shivering,
                                an instant chilled!—

And from the mute powers of the sky, like the swift
shape of dolphin or perhaps the husk of rage,
something gray like thunder dives into stone,
catapulted out of the centuries, a split second warp
of time tearing itself loose!—in an ungoverned country…
beyond the time-locked vaults, the steel-hearted banks.

Inherit the night the evicted workers whose lives were
used up, whose bodies broke down or were broken,
or the murdered conscripts who died in wars not theirs,
locating in the wind that shuffles its pauses and patience
with cards the dead own,
                        wind rising with the brooding

shadows in the cities where the people are yanked by
alarms toward work,
                    and the generals who dreamed
something awful under the burning stars,
                             a ghostly
wrath diving into stone,
                    rise to reclaim power.

And the day opens again with the absence heavy,
the assaulting light, arrives without those *others,*
citizens who didn't survive yesterday's war or rent:
become the weather or our own exile, become
the emptiness who dines on our discontents, become
our severities,
                the wind tearing at our money,
the future a bankrupt place and the past a forgotten one—
or the other way around.
                  The hour of daybreak is
the structures of steel and wood resurrecting themselves
out of the soft light of our sleep,
                  the city gathering
its energies as its citizens order their world as their owners
have ordered them—and from mechanical habit the city
falls into motion, without knowing itself or its history—

Yesterday's newspaper walks the wind like a ragged dancer

while the wind gnaws without word at the edges of the world.

                        * * * * *

...became the lost world of swirling ashes mourning itself,
joyous world murdered,
                  the cities transported to fiery
legends inscribed upon the sky, the smoke of the bombed
districts,
            those of the poor always, or the smoke

of the factories our lives feed daily for a myth of freedom
never ours,
              while our government extends its terrors—
and the wind, which knows the hollowness of sea shells
polished smooth,
                  gathers up the smashed remains…

    And it was wind that called me
    out of myself, opening my way:
    from the snow-locked fields of March,
    singing of the people who knew
    wind's desolations, bringing me
    their news, out of the earth, long
    struggle, their happenings become
    collected aria, rootless elegies,
    the relentless and ragged story
    of our need…in the halls of wind
    one world calling—out of the distance
    as I knew distance was built into
    our hearts, the fate of the poor
    together—a house without walls…

"…the ancient cry for bread" while the wind lifts
the fragrance of roses,
                         incites the dawn birds,
over the cities the wings weaving—
                              primordial song…
ancient cry…
            oracular with time…
                              free…
in the wind that transcends litigation:
                              wind that swept
through the ruins of vague capitols sunken into the hills,
ancient empires,
              voices of workers the wind's chorus,
fallen guerrillas,
              all who lost fighting against loss,

fallen
farmers against the old order,
Shay's rebels against
losing the Revolution when bible-prayer-country
answered only with strict law,
voices multiplied
out of gun smoke and hunger...
isolations multiplied,
coming together like a hollow wound in the sound
of the wind,
a cry in the night,
and the light unwoven
by the wings of hunting nighthawks yields the world
to the complaints of the past where all days are withered
inside a dead rose:
their skies heavy:
impecunious
workers with only the pennies of their eyes infinite,
bathed in the dissolving harsh lunar light,
in the consuming
dark...
their cold distances become the distance
to ourselves,
the wind's measure of an ancient grief...

* * * * *

We've been to the place where the moon stretches its soul
upon the river...
at the beginning...
and the stars that shaped two fish shone there also.

Neither lunar river nor its guardian trees have changed—
but we've changed and been changed, under the cosmic
ceiling of our own Dream,
the stars like silent time-keepers
awaiting the time of our voice, the one traveling commune

our home the world the wind travels—or our exile…

And the fishes etched in the night in their house eternally
drifting toward spring and sleeping their nuptial dream
of sadness in the waterless realm in their cosmic silence
cannot guide us home from this age of Hiroshima when
80 thousand deaths were instantly lifted to incineration
under the sign of one spark!—
                          a tiny flicker against space,
one city-star on earth that blazed us
                              into the nuclear cradle:
pileus of ash pitiless building its momentary candescence
like an exploding skull mocking the sun at dawn.

We've been to the forum and the park—
                          angry,
then tired,
          then seasoned,
                          protesting what the seasons
themselves have scorned,
                      or grieved—the dust migrating
from the exploited earth…
                      we protested what the winds
could not forget even while we slept, the dust a gathering
army that walked across the continent, in the Thirties
black horizons closing upon us like our own nightmares,
as if the earth itself commanded we speak the word
we've yet to mouth:
                      our own lost voice like a wind-worn
cry that begins itself over out of exhausted vowels,
out of midnight's throat, again and again out of the ashes
that end in the rivers, out of the sacrificial ledgers
that calculate profits and leave the barren confines
of charred rubble—
                      or bodies dumped at the city's edge.

Now the old struggles intensify their meanings…

the terrors come naked as the empire expands!
With shark teeth extorted from the warehouses of the sea
they smile at us speaking their deadly lies, the bosses
expanding their wars, all the corrupt politicians and CEOs,
money-mongers with their death squads, the President
"the Great Communicator" making peace with dead fascists
in Bitburg, Germany—salesman of agonies resurrecting
the tormentors—or the Great Pretender, Bush the Minor
declaring perpetual war on U.S. democracy,

                                  the great

terrorists of the world speak

                      and the flowers flame like
the sun's dwellings,

                like the judgment of martyrs,
each blind hour denied the poor—

                     flowers the mortal
cathedrals of the murdered who refuse to die, whose
betrayed dawns the birds sing:

                    "each of us is a country
destroyed…we are the people without money or words
by which to live…

             who return homeless by the seasons…"

…calling out of ourselves,

              the wind of our own lost voice,
calling the moment when meaning touches our shadows
coming

       together…

            listening for the whisper of *a word*
through the grasses…

             perhaps a sea sound in the wind—
coming from a long ways away,

             through the ages—
a word or its music or the feeling of *freedom*—

              in how many

languages?—
                    perhaps even *love*?…
                                        our shadows joining
in a dream day when our bodies
                            can praise…
                                        distance…

III.

Hunting My Home Town

They come to dig up the plant
They come to defile the child
Through misery and weariness.

-Paul Eluard

Think of the depressing contrast
between the radiant intelligence of
a healthy child and the feeble
intellectual powers of the average adult.

-Sigmund Freud

Dale Jacobson

.

1.

Nascent,
      dazzling the days I remember,
my home town where I spent my youth—
and not since has the light been so steadfast or precise,
cast upon the ecumenical corn,
                  the sky-tinged fields
of intoxicating alfalfa,
              the shadowy wizardly hawthorn
that tutored its roots through the rocks, in the ditches
the robust and roguish ragweed named for its leaves.

Nor since have I known so well the dark furies in the earth
with hearts of rose quartz:
                dark dark energies the evening
air released,
        the breeze suffused with the earth's solitary
sadness,
      mute,
         powerful—
            legacy of ancestors—

the roads that led out to the wild plums and chokecherries
that deepened like eyes in the dark...

From the elemental mysteries accumulating
terrestrial time, the matrix of stone, the strata
of minerals where the geological weathers meditate,
the garden of marine fossils dreamed with a thirst
like dry thunder the lost sea lifted into the sky—

then!—
      (even as the earth voyaged through echoless space),
by fire and water that transform each other into ascending
wings turning on the void, I climbed the spiraling ladder
of the blood's codes, the genetic language that spoke

out of its own dying, the cry of earth and air—I came
by the occult metaphors manifest in the elements
whose sum is life, whose energies govern our senses,
and by which sense arrives…

Animal yearning to become human…

I listened for the words to name a world which,
born nameless like myself, was equal under
the equal light…
                free…
                        neither owned nor sold…
my own young bones like the sturdy slender popples,
grown from the timeless, time-keeping earth…

By words, when words came together,
I was saved from the anonymous terrors—
the emptiness of the moon among the shadows
and the rivers leaning into their estuaries—
even inside the deep solitary vowels of the dark wind,
all the voices of the Many slept in the maternal lull.

In my bedroom with the western window toward the town
I thought of all the drifting dreamers who had made
the day mighty—called to their internal and stored light
under the journeying moon in its womb of luminous silence
over the empty lamp-guarded streets…

The city I sought—
                to which we all belonged—
                                and still
belong—was not the one I would come to know, later,
when words went away,
                        seemed to sink into their own
autumnal grieving, or the sad marrow of my bones.

Through the halls of school, long tunnel of those years,

I learned the hardness of speech and my own silence,
words always hunting for the victim—words become
malicious from being denied grief, given the sense
of the knife but not the wound—when I learned time
was money and my own time condemned to a terrifying
meditation of words locked in my head—murdered words
no one would or could hear, in a city dying to be invented—
stilled—
   enduring itself—
      city bereaved of itself—
no more free than the hands of its workers…

Came the way of our ancestors…
        searching the mythic,
still unmade city located on the rumor the wind transports…

the wandering commune—
     lost—
       nomadic—

from following the rivers…

Came to the human and inhumane history of my nation,
preceded by the Indians now ghostly dancing the tribal
commune,
   their flint arrowheads locked in the rock—
preceded by those whose rivers belonged to another
continent:
   "a ghost wanders through Europe…that ghost
is communism"—
     as I wandered my home town,
         from
the wandering of my ancestors I came,
      seeking among seekers

the language the earth yearns to yield and build, the only way
it knows:
        by blood,
            trial,
                 work—struggle…by the needs
of breath:

      this is how the blind furies
      rise up to give birth to our voice:

      inside each word all our ghostly cries!

2.

Lama sabachthani—
                    this was life forsaken,
                                        in my growing,
all the more tragic because it was mine! Crucifixion
without need of the cross,
                            which burned someplace else,
like the light come into the world the crosses of Christian
pyromaniacs
            chosen
                        by the color of their skin,
by the color of their God, by the color of death
in pale robes,
            to offend—
                        or murder—
whomsoever of any other color offendeth their eyes!

To this country I came, like everyone came
unknown from nowhere, with no memory came
out of the commerces of the past, the dark distances,
the continuum of night falling into night—and each day
rising up like a small bright journey from the center
of the body's emptiness toward—
                            a world—
beyond the continent of the sleeping hand.

In the morning of my questions I sought the city
(something like a circle), but in the evening of
terrible answers, which were glowering silences
under the brows of the adults, I ended sullen
as a recluse rushing toward a reckless solitude!

Our small town huddled together under the street lights,
encompassed within the legions of corn whose dark rustle
was haunted by the Indians of the last century

121

whose lives still inhabited the prairie—
this tiny town
under the turning galaxies was not saved or safe from
the old struggles.
> City of my growing…
transmutational
soil…
> where I invented my earliest maps,
city of light
once—
> of failing light I couldn't levitate—
city of
my sleeping angers born from the nightmare past.

Out of the old world.
> The old wars.
Anger like
a black rose closed upon secret lightnings—
lingers still—
a ferocious melancholy this city of far distances to itself!

To the wreckage of a language I was born, language
of mirages and dreams barren as a nation without water,
a nation of desperate distances from the poor—
born—
to this provincial town on the prairie of the nation
whose guardian angel or lost angelic guard
stares blind into the past, sentinel of the gates
of the financial Eden of the East, the Big Apple,
where the futures (of workers) are bought and sold,
the casino stock exchange of the fixed wheel of fate:

> *Give me your homeless that I might make homeless.*
> *Give me your hungry that I might make hungry.*
> *Give me your poor that I might make poor.*

> And in the ancient dungeon,

or the dark dream-cell of discontents,
the slave holds vigil—or the worker:
waiting for the visions
to appear on the stone walls,
remembrances of cave paintings,
when the commune danced!

But no visions appear, no new words are spoken, no one
is freed.
       The dark bird soars off into the summer sky…

And so I learned not to speak (children better seen
than heard) in this town where no one talked—
and at school only bravado, the braggadocio of
Norwegian bull-fighters, sang the class song!

There I stood against the wall of the hallway, each free
time, watching the Great Society, in the armor of my
silence,
       weaponless—wondering when play had become
verbal fray—
           serious—
                desperate—the play of power while
among the powerless and wearied young, suicide called.

The old oak against the prairie sky
cast its slight shadow over
the young corn
in the mid afternoon July sun.
On its dead branch a crow
seemed to doze.
I was fifteen, the age when
I had first imagined
suicide, my empty chair
in the classroom, my classmates
speaking through my absence.
I drew my bow. Let fly the arrow.

Missed. The crow lifted, a shadow,
a flurry like a dark tunnel
through the air! Gone.
The startled fierce eyes!
This was no holy ghost,
wasn't about to be nailed to a tree.
I envied its leaving…

Because I couldn't.
       Couldn't leave.
             Couldn't hitchhike
south to join Huck Finn as I had tried when I was twelve.
To find him and Jim—friends. Float the river.
The innocence of my years to continue. Couldn't.

And escape the anger and the laws of the adults
who hated their own slavery in a country they called free.

Their own sacrifice.
       They hated.
            And their children
who didn't want the world they themselves didn't want
they forgot to find.
       Their own lives lost to the boss.

No—
     the punished past would not cease to suffer
and would not suffer alone, would not forget those
who refused to change it—despite the nondepartment
of nonrecognitions that recognized only
the nonrecognition of all suffering not ordained
or divine, despite the heavenly and blissful
lack of conscience or consciousness while the nation
shipped the youth of its poor off to war,
and the draft board decided who was expendable
and who was not, nevertheless, the punished past
continued to punish the present, obeyed its own

recognitions like the winds that would not cease—
and the body bags came back despite the giving death
two thousand years old, the moon continued in its orbit,
the rivers refused to flow backwards, the fundamental
particles continued their fundamental arrangements:

    water : earth : fire :   air—and in us:
     /   /   /   /
    dream : labor : voice : spirit…

To these elements I was born—at harmony in themselves
though sundered and at war in us—from and to
their powers I came:
                  their occult analogies contemporised
in the mathematical loom of the interweaving physics—
from and to the elements I came without memory
to a strange country which could hardly talk to itself—
though I almost heard—
                far away…
like a correspondence from the future weaving through
the wind,
         a choir of children singing an old language,
until I heard again the winds worry through the weeds
with the hollow voices of the nation's dead.

I was born to a country governed by its own ashes
sown upon the wind like griefs, from the first Indian
village outward—
        to Viet Nam—
             to Nicaragua—
to: the cities manufacturing the death weapons,
and the homeless employed by terror and need,
hunting the streets,
        "gathering fuel in vacant lots"
while the world revolves like ancient women grieving
for their children's children…and garbage can furnaces
brighten the alleys, the national flag fixed on the moon.

I was born to the hierarchical and hieratic histories,
the fiery crosses, which did not signify the *axis mundi*
where all forces converge, not the ancient cross *saltire*
that brings thunder and rain, nor the *crux dissimulata*
signifying the four winds, nor the Celtic cross or
the *kiakra* signifying sexual union, the phallus and yoni,
which Christianity made into a grave marker,
nor the yin and yang the cross of dialectics,
nor the Cross *Fourchée*, the branching tree.

But I was born to the cross of forks transformed in fire,
flowering in flames, the cross of the Ku Klux Klan,
stolen from the Scottish cross of alarm, the call to war.
It was the "x" of power's singular logic where time and space
collapse in someone's death—especially anyone not of
the Aryan Club.
                    Though I didn't then know,
in the eternal town of my childhood, what I needed
and wanted—
                    dying to live—
                              still,
                                    out of the gullies,
valleys,
          ravines and hills—
                              the fields I wandered—
out of the land I invoked my ancestors like a family
from a fallen time,
                    touching the commune on the wind
they haunted,
              the dead,
                        those who had known the land,
pioneers and Indians whose far lives through the land
were connected to mine,
                        somehow made me feel
at home,
          their benign vicinity—

even nurturing—
who had returned to the elemental dark.

So I went: imagining (like Yeats) in some better faring past
the far lost human family—while those for whose company
I yearned, my schoolmates, went as I did—lost further
in their moment—disconnected—took refuge in cynicism—
learning to lose—trying to learn futility—all of us traveling
toward the future dead…of Viet Nam.

Mine was the city where *someone* in the last light was lost—
and is still—
        in the stillness *another* boy I'll never know
who might have (easily—once) praised all the free senses!—
or it is the city of another country of this boy I *was*—once—
in the intense and brief, free morning bright…
that country all children know before they learn
to disappear within their skins…
                shields on their eyes…
protecting internal spaces, dark rooms where the nostalgias
are poisonous shade plants that live on the dead days.

It came to pass the light away,
          the city,
            the moment
we learned to sell ourselves,
            to surrender the powerful
complacencies of summer,
          its serene and handsome,
resplendent sun-shouldering hills—
            and the city that was
once ours calcified into a memory that hardened further,
layered inside the pristine gloaming never again known—
lost to the hungry darkness we would come to haunt:
at the Blue Moon where we drank to await the war
that awaited our arrival—
         from home:

furious and delirious drunken dilly-dally of the damned!

And I drank and drank and drank and drank and drank!

How I failed or was failed comes down at last to:
the wounds of class that are graduated upon
the preposition prepostured upon my confusion
and showered by confabulatory confetti at the fool's
ball game warden outpost where we skin them alive
and bet our lives and kick the stuffing out of a long shot
when in the curse of inhuman events the better to knock
them dead unvindicted in the Good War!—where so many
of us were headed after homecoming from over there...
hunting my home town—
                          hunting...

City located in the translunar,
                          transmogrified,
                                    unyielding
hour of adult despairs!
                          Since then I 've seen the great cities,
Chicago, New York, London, Paris...

                          And came to see
the blazing fiery windows of the financial fortresses
looming tall over our toil,
                          their chandelier light like
captured constellations,
                          their fountains in the ornate
foyers—
            all our energy and time in those great architectures
all beyond our hands that build the sky plazas...while
our
      darker elevators
                  go only down!

Somewhere in the funereal heavens of poverty,

or in the bright death of Nuclear Midnight,
the cities of children wane into another orbit—
lost for the future envisioned by bankers,
they who have purchased the Apocalypse,
who have launched an infinite graph of profits
into space, who see only by the black light
of their own planet's dying aura:

    when the expropriated wealth
    reaches critical mass,
    all cities *must* shift—

    by mass revolution or:
    by the lifting flames
    of swift skeletal birds!

And so:
      out of the wind that erases its steps as it arrives,
and out of the slant of rain—
                or the dusky and dark soil
where the moths of autumn have fallen through
the colors of summer,
          out of the enduring elements—
if *we* endure—
      we come—
          hunting our home towns,
we of the working class who survive hard times—
              or don't—
who survive deadly times—
      or don't—
survive the fatal times to which no one belongs—
           or don't—
survive…
      But if we survive the silence that accepts
no names, but endures only itself—if we survive
enough
    to endure

all indifferences, we must make
a difference—
for ourselves.

Must do what survival
requires beyond itself to make survival worthwhile.

Out of so much survival must be conceived the invention,
the words exchanged,
the rite of passage to the singing gates
of the four horizons,
from our far blind wanderings
passage to the human circle ancient within us,
like the Stonehenge dolmens storing the stars,
gathering the millennial light,
open to all comers,
all these centuries long…
free:
the lost city—
ours:
time and space recognized for what they are,
a method for
our discovery—
of each other—
by which we begin
to see…

3.

(departure)

The wind ushers me back
to those trees swaying
in their high precincts of light,
elms and poplars on Pine Street,
and the gravel road leading from town
past the cemetery to the fields of corn
condensing the sun into kernels
by an alchemy of cool green flames and silken smoke.

In that one and only childhood country,
in my backyard garden of potatoes and zenias
my meditational hands learned
the damp humus where the husk
of the seed decays for the seed
to be born—and beyond:
my feet learned the pathways,
the formal concrete sidewalks
and the informal shortcuts worn
into the grass—those trails
that seemed then timeless as legends or rain.

I listened for the place names,
the lakes of Marshall, Canby, Cottonwood,
the rocky shores of rough Lake Shetak...

There at the waters we kids gathered
to give our words away by the sound of waves,
the crickets knitting the dusk into night:
but then, the campfire stones, charred and cracked,
became a vacant mouth of ashes without use—
the ashes gone, the stones gone, the waters the same,
at the shores the weeping willows

whose phantom hair the stars descend—

Those fires are defunct, their shadows
departed—the twine of smoke like memory
has climbed the all-effacing sky.

The echoes of that country call,
which I once knew by clearer vision,
the town our words made shine!—
where we brightened a land that was
never ours—
                    already lorded except for
the subtle musics we there contrived:

>   in tomorrow's long ruins
>   let me never forget
>   those voices sovereign
>   in nomadic time…

My home town, though gone
to ultra-interior fame,
is *not* innocence reduced
to the residue of cynical carbon,
a remote country burned away
by the harsher light of this land
I've come to know ruled by war.

—But calls now out of an older history
than my small loss.

Come wind come wings come world
come war come ruins come dust
come hunger—city—empire
come flag come dust come hunger
come city come moon come world
come grief come wrath come words
come home workers come together

come the commune come into the streets—
song of hands this song sings!

And each day arrives as then
belonging entirely to itself
without debt or mortgage,
the steady swift light
which to itself is free!—
the same since the beginning,
awaiting the opening of our eyes,
awaiting the same revolution
all these centuries long!

4.

Let this then child unfreed still
reside homeless at home inside
these my eyes that have become
further distanced than the decades…
and come accustomed to see

this world born from the cosmic ash
it is—not as the pyre-mongers would
brighten it who hunt our home towns
with fires their madness has long ruled—
but as I know my home town

has always been ash of some
far exploded instant-engine
which weaving time conceived into
this earth we sort of know, sorting out
the possibles—this world we might

transform and make into another:
shape of star we are, blazing
more brightly than light: our home
towns and cities built of words
among the workers who proclaim or shall

our day raised up by a legacy of
our losses: song of our wind returning
that shall give this star-world birth,
much brighter yet than that
dream-city some child-ancient built…

IV.

Calling Back the Fire Bird

Dale Jacobson

1.

There are moments when I'm afraid to pause—
when I feel gravity like a column of zeros
falling through themselves...

                  all calculations lost...
no direction...
        condemned to circling...

And so I sing the finale of this long cry...
Two decades gone—like the sweeping swoosh
of a swift hawk's shadow!
                And still, cryptic
in the dust, isolated in its name, the name of America...
What an old land it was I came to haunt!

A country unknown—for all its books! For all its colonies
and conquered peoples! The past buried and the future
an avalanche poised to collapse, a perdition of fatigued
tomorrows and their dreams fallen through the bottom
of hope like the prophecy of a dead archeologist—

The national debt.
        The national grief,
                turned inward—
need crushing itself like a black hole, like our reflections
in the window panes we stare beyond—or hope to—
but lose ourselves in the vista where the land or
city-scapes forget what our lives have not become...
the image of ourselves staring back like a ghost
caught in the glass—
           looking for a way back into
our lives—hunting...
           a place that knows us.

But love seems a makeshift bed where money rules the stars.

We've come the longest journey, the longest way, through
the darkly-dearsome and wearied young years when
no one would, or could, answer our callings—voices
of our hungers,
                  charred lands,
                              ashen flora of childhood,
twentieth century children cast into chaos,
                                    into the next
millennium,
            like those before cast into their tomorrows…
those smoky years where someone is still wandering alone—
"who did we leave behind?"—dim faces with fear for eyes,
or angry hurts, vengeful nostalgias that go on living,
haunting our long since lost places—in the back yard
an indistinct mournful bowed shape,
                            or near the river—
"who was never allowed to speak?"—while we turn
like shadow-dials from moon to dawn as the old empire
turns for war:
              I came…
                    I saw…
                        I wept…

our lives of youth hunting love wasted
as the hunting guns wasted nameless lives…

Ever since I stepped out my front door to go to school
and walked down the street, I've been hunting
another country unnamed fallen through the stars…
in another dimension if I could find it—a world worth
stepping into—
                  I sought to climb the lunar water filament
of the sunken dream world, to waken to the jay cry and
cool breeze in the lateral early light.
                          How do I unspell
the name of America, how do I dispel its name to the wind,

what spell could I cast into the wind against its history?

And when I walked into my twenties, the future
that unfolded sanctified to meet me was the war
on foreign hills, while the ghost of my past had long
been orphaned, become my tyrant without a country,
calling out of loss with my younger voice, somewhere
located on the wind beneath which the corn fields
had been stolen and the summer from the honey.

It had been a long journey to the massacre!

Always I've hunted my home town—
                              wandering
the roads by which we map our time—I came longing
for many voices that would build the city of song!—
came to those I met along the way, taking note
of the blue flags in the ditches, wild irises
folding the sky's splendor into their blossoms,
their sexual capitals—
                              enchanted airy cupolas…
or taking note of the night birds that themselves
sing in voices that are blue: out of the wind-rising
memory of the day's oneness and passing, populated
solitude singing!—
                    inside the eternal void, which is
something else and the same, but absolute…

Our time together must mean more than time lost…
and speak together another kind of memory or survival—
and bring together need and loss in the electromagnetic
disciplines of NOW!—
                         as we came together briefly during
the war against the war.
                         From out of the past that leans
like a knife toward the indifferent habits of rust,
                                        all tools

gnawed by their vanquishing sunsets,
.   in that strange
dimming light where memory lives in the country we lost,
I wondered as we wandered our roads to each day's end
where our country went, how under the stars to call it back.

But our songs came slightly, like vaporous choirs in the rain,
hesitant—or didn't come at all: came as bitter voices—
dry, resentful,
                    touching the world only like the wings
of dead dragonflies,
                        lost out of time…
                                            whispers…
maybe mumblings in sleep no one heard, not even
ourselves.
                After the war we forgot the world.

Though we didn't know it then, tomorrow was already
lost even as we won the war against the war,
                                            briefly—
but tomorrow arrived unchanged, already exploited
and exhausted,
                    leaving the poor changeless,
                                            broke,
broken—
            lost in the empire like the American Dream
is lost,
        the national memory a mirage like a glass
spellbound and gyrating round its own column
of water: in which are revealed like fantastic refractions
visions of "the good old days"—a thirst for times
that never existed, the fountain of youth, and patriotism
galore!—
            nationalism reborn!—
                                flag country and country
music unlimited!—the rasping voices of a Roman dream:
"May Caesar with justice rule and God's lightning strike

the polluted woods" where the heathens hide!

I stepped out of my front door into the twentieth century
and out onto the dangerous roads, the electric guitars
shaped from the lightning of the times called—
Jimi Hendrix playing to the flame!
                                                            Alive!—

                                                                        voices…
voices…
                        briefly…
                                    Jim Morrison calling from
the wilderness of the insane children called to war:

    Cancel my subscription to the resurrection.
    Send my credentials to the house of detention.

Those roads then took me down a dark funeral,
Viet Nam on fire,
                        the dead leaping from their caskets
to be killed again and again!—and my own raging fires
wrapping me round like incandescent visions
in which I saw the bodies falling, faces warped out of time,
the tenants of tormented space—
                                                these dead and dying
still fixed there:
                        in the memory of the pain my nation
inflicted,
                they return to us, and return us to our
hurt and harm,
                        our country's savagery written in its law:
in profit and private poverty we trust—e pluribus unum.

Those gone into the smoke return us to confrontation
like the letter *C* circles upon the gap of itself—
the class struggle of:
                        the broken commune—
which can't keep out the winds of the discontented past.

Dale Jacobson

All roads like destiny return to the place where
the circle was first made unwhole, unholy,
where Dumnacus lost at the converging four rivers,
Les Ponts-de-Ce, and Spartacus,
                                        Stepan Razin,
Crazy Horse,
                Anna Mae Aquash,
                                Joe Hill,
Rosa Luxemburg,
                        Zapata,
                                Martin Luther King,
Viola Liuzzo,
                Farabundo Marti,
                                Karen Silkwood,
Annie Lo Pizzo: many names—martyred and
many more names forgotten—fallen into history
with the Disappeared, the demolished alphabet…

It was the letter *C* of class I sought to rename with the older
C—sign of the sickle which once cut the Communal grain,
shape of the quarter moon journeying toward
the full hour of harvest, shining like a sliver of knowledge,
the *C* with the ghost of the circle behind it, with
the community of dead workers watching our world
through its dark portal: the hollow silent ones
in the circular night waiting for the lucid luminous rising
of the past rounding the horizon…
                                to come home.

2.

Out of the prairie intoxicated with torpor
under the odors of sweet clover and alfalfa,
out of my sentient silence I came to Moorhead,
in 1970,
        looking for a way
                to demolish and abolish
the country of childhood locked in dream-fixed-light
of a dream dreaming a dream that couldn't walk
out of itself, still-born loneliness,
                in the labyrinthine
streets of that remote town of Marshall:
                    empty
footfalls,
        wandering the edge of the wind, the child
of myself wandering the hilly prairie among rocks
like stone birds folded into themselves,
                  a closed world…

Leaving the Redwood River opening south
for the northward flowing river of the Red, migration
toward the latitudes where the Aurora Borealis builds
its scaffolding of light,
            I went wildering always
on the edge of five dollars and one horizon,
which only the poor know—
              circling the circle of poverty
and meditating upon the stormy governments
of the high ionic cities,
            invoking the powers,
imperative of lightning shedding its husk of thunder
like collapsing corrugations, natural law which still
convenes above our injudicious one, rain whose
rhythms insisted that my own barren summers
blossom into the world—

with or without joy.

I came to Moorhead where Tom McGrath
carried his poetry like a small moon,
a companion sphere of light floating at his side
and there—
                    in that working-class town, the literary
renaissance of Minnesota was born,
                                        briefly!

Its energies lasted for about half of five seconds—
or the life of a firefly in the pitch black night—
came pure like the supernal Kindred Lights legendary—
rumored by local myth makers—
                              ·   lights of kin—
wide roamers of exile on the prairie,
                                  eerie emanations
that floated out of their dark caves of air
like luminous globes of lost spirits drifting
through the trees,
                    over the river,
                              and outward toward
the vast Dacotah Territory—
                        and then gone!—
ignis fatui—
          will-o-the-wisps—
                        or displaced dreams of
older inhabitants
              buoyed over the history of the land…

We were also lost and kindred spirits haunting
or haunted by the outlawed ghost-dancing past:
the writers from Moorhead, who walked the black
waters of the Red River—
                    restless—
                              witnesses
of a dying empire—

the Unhappy, the Wounded—
we went into grief, we went into anger, we went
into distance, we went inventing our own light
to live by:
    the comradery,
                bonhomie,
                        sodality
of the lost...
            when with clemency we endured
wrangling and shindy between us to cease,
on a good day, if the wind were calm.

And sad Pisces reigned in the black heavens of cold
shale, where the stars were fixed in the ritual of time
that ruins the wronged by the wars of the rulers.

And even as we murmured, shouted and purled
our homing calls for a home that daily slipped
further away into dusky memory, other
(wiser loftier) poets who contemplated the aesthetics
of protest with the convictions of their silence,
the counter-counter culture poets who could count
money but not bodies, recited their confessions
consummate and capricious enthusiasms passionate—and
in the half-life of their words fell a rain of dead moths
beneath which the anger of the land was buried!

And the grand-old-pome-shysters made a lofty profession
of elevated euphoria glittering like Buffalo Bills or Janes
on the side-show stage coach stuck in Romantic Dream
Porch County, scintillation of the poets' used-verbs circus,
they who would sell their mother's tongue for cash!—
I've listened to field mice at 5 a.m. chatting in the grass
who are poets of higher order than those ingravescent
pause makers prissy—
                profoundly heavy—
with two tons of leaden sleep in their voices—

145

they who came to tame the Indians again with new
treatises of nuance:

     sic transit gloria mundi—

that's the way

    it goes

      down…

the language of the poor sold out—

        silenced!

But…

   in Moorhead for an instant in monolithic city,
something happened: something like a long chill
that sang down our spines, or perhaps a cry so shrill
it became a thin crystal telepathy threaded on wind,
seeking its primal syllable, the terrible silence of:
the far murdered exploring in us their absence.

Inaugurated our words.

      These foreign dead who were
also our own on foreign soil: the dead of all nations
equal.

   The fatal light of napalm streaking the skies
over Viet Nam like a dream inside the skull of a corpse,
wakened our young eyes to an older age, the new
fire rain like the Fourth of July,

       the old war against

the secret Unions of Water—

      the Peoples of Water we all are.

Uncle Death of the Long Beard pointed his gaunt finger
from an arm draped in a shroud of bloody stripes,
the stars nailed in their blue regiment, the universe
ordered—and down the horizons the nation's white
winds of destruction swept, evicted the poor from
their lives, conscripted their blood for the raven eyes
of General Westmoreland, whose name defined the deed.

Others like Fred Hampton were executed in their sleep
by the police in Daley's Chicago, as the police still do,
killing 80 year old women in New York with shotguns—
or 15 year old kids in Iowa with twelve pistol shots,
in their homes—or bombing their homes in Philadelphia:

>*"Behold, I have set before you*
>*an open door, which no one*
>*is able to shut"*—made of ashes
>and the charred bones of children...

And the American Legionnaires, more patriotic than
starched uniforms are stiff: "Why don't they go live
in Russia if they don't like their deaths here?"

"Go..."
        "Leave..."—we heard who were here born—
and we went—
                Indian-like—
                                back: into the anger
of the land—
        Corpus Mater Universalis.

It was then, in an incendiary season...while
the farmers were planting the earth with seed,
who continued losing their farms, and the National
Guard was planting the campuses with the bodies
of students, and the churches were singing
each Sunday into oblivion to forget the daily dead
of that far country where our President ravaged.

Like the coruscation of the Aurora Borealis,
those far villages in flame transformed our town:
we became mavericks inventing our own dance
on the horizons of ruined time, in a time when
all the grandfather clocks dreamed in the shape
of vertical coffins, when time was money and

money was death, and my German grandfather
(who fought against the Kaiser in World War I) said:
"I wouldn't fight in that god-damned dirty war,"
shocking my uncle his son who hated draft dodgers
and wanted to drop the atomic bomb, in that war
where Menschfresser Nixon raged in his martyrdom
of wealth and power like a bulldog weeping,
even as his teeth tore at Wounded Knee,
at the throats of mothers and their young at My Lai.

Under the summer sun the prairie of perpetual fields
shimmering, its terrain like an immense freedom, seemed—
and the spacious calm inhabited the wide wheat while
the red winged blackbirds chattered in the ditches.

We outcasts of outcasts,
                    cast out of the *Outcast Club*
which outlawed the outlaw rivers,
                                we outriders sought
the city lost outside of time, whose lights we tried
to invoke or invent like *the Kindred Lights of all Kin*
out of our need to locate on wind or wild wish
the myth of our home town,
                        under the stars
of the prairie,
            the wide cities of the universal night
we sought by pure sorcery of words to reclaim fire,
call up from the ashes of the alphabet,
                                from
the language of war,
                "the far fires of the fugitive past,"
the fire-bird that had once leapt from hand
into hammer into steel and finally leapt from
sky over the cities,
                all that labor become death—
all that fire passed through our hands, workers
who through the centuries chiseled from the ores

of night the starry hieroglyphs,
                              hollow and cold
fires in the vast deep,
                    in the still undeciphered
nightmare heavens where all dead are equal.

3.

Winter.
    From East Grand Forks I look back over
that now ghostly and fallow, unsudden, suddenly
hallowed terrain, belonging to its hollow, nebulous
light—
    look back to Moorhead and further to Marshall,
with an eye locked in lazer gaze, memory's strange
time-traveling lightwaves that enlarge by whimsy.

Huge to say: from there I came here!—but knowing
myself at last among the shadow-dancing poor.

And here is where?—on the map of legal thievery,
national rip-off lane, highway robbery, abstract art
of usury and shakedown, the high law of imperialism
for low filching, cold conceptual cannibalism!

In a country where *freedom* is an immense word,
the freedoms are immensely small. Look how small
is freedom:
        one half of one per cent own one third
of the nation's wealth—while one quarter of nation's
children live in poverty...
                        fractions of lives...
fragmented country...
                ghettos...
                    slums...

Reagan Ranches...
            Bush's thousand points of light,
Clinton's war on the poor,
                    Bush the Pretender's
perpetual war against any terrorism not his own
(to make the world safe for nuclear holocaust).

The same.
             Justice the same. Injustice the same.
The war on the poor the same. The F.B.I. the same
led by the same Richard Held of the Chicago Raids in '68—
of the Wounded Knee siege in 73—and in the tradition of
the Palmer Raids of the 20s, the F.B.I. unleashes itself
against the Independistas of Puerto Rico, protecting
the rich ports of the rich, (no independence from the laws
the Justice Department breaks!)—as says Attorney General
scam-man Meese: "sending a signal to terrorists and their
supporters…" or Attorney General for Christ Ashcroft—

When the terrorists speak of terror, we know nothing
has changed—hands.
                      In the hands of the poor,
nothing remains,
                which is the same,
                                  hands without
change—
             no transmutation of fate.
                                The poor who hold
no power in their hands, except to cease—to gather
the defeats of all the world, who can hold night
like a pool a curled shadow an abyss dark coin
in the palm of the hand and refuse to lift the world—
who can make something out of nothing by making
nothing—a still storm whose face is fierce…

                        * * * * *

I remember the street lamps blazing unchanged
like mourners bowed in a frozen cathedral, along
the wintery streets while the fire rain continued
to fall over Viet Nam, through my twenties while
I walked among the silent houses of Moorhead
where half the year we had to move fast to keep

from icing up, in the long glacial light blue under
the moon: in the snow bank hotel of Norwegian cold!

And there all seemed paralyzed,
                              a world alone of lonely
people, citizens of a kakistocracy turning their grief
toward no belief,
                    caught in a nihilistic nightmare,
wandering within the glacial fence of the moraines,
a landlocked katabasis,
                        a retreat never won…

The most difficult place on earth to leave,
like a hobo camp built from despair, no place
better worth going to,
                        the stock market wheeling
and dealing as the nation reeled—under
the after-shock of bombs curving earthward
a half world and unconsciousness away, on the night
side of the mind—
                    and business booming!

Some walked deeper into the Red River valley, forgot
to stop going
            down—
                    walked into the deep underground
misty caverns, the long trip toward exotic Asian or
South American plant life: carnivorous—fell into their own
winter of drugs, a private season cold that captured them
like a glow in the snow that closed the cellar door.

Underground economy in a country of no jobs…
                                        and

in Washington, D.C.,
                    a covert economy for the C.I.A.—
later to become Reagan's "just say no" war on the drugs
he himself, who himself knew nothing of what he did,
was dealing:
                    democracy at work: drugs here for guns there,
against Nicaragua,
                    where the Viet Nam War had moved—
which was the war we were fighting then—to end.

We seem to be going in circles…
                    a perpetual war,
(as Bush the Pretender would later call it) with its
perpetual and caught dead,
                    the *C* of continuous
confrontation,
                    class struggle (which doesn't exist),
one world under someone else's idea of God—
those streets paved in gold for someone else's feet,
where Christ continues to do the washing—
and no the horizons from dawn to dusk are free.

And there in Moorhead, during that other same war,
we were prisoners of our own voices that climbed
the midnight slant of an askew moon, like maverick
coyotes—
                    in a twilight zone—
                              Moorhead on the frontiers
of stasis!
                    It was the center of nowhere in particular,
which was flat and circled itself and always returned
without another destiny,
                    as the Indians of the last
Minnesota war knew: the Sugar Point Battle warriors
in Moorhead imprisoned: where all good ends—end.

Dale Jacobson

The sadness of the place was heavier than the fuscuos clay,
the color of dusk,
                 on which the city was built—
constructed O U T ward where no U P would dare,
and plenty of OUT was there,
                       though the people
kept trying to find it—out,
                   the way out of being left out—
of work,
        or love (which seemed to go best with money),
hunting the way out of out—
                 way out—the furthest out
farther than "far out"—
              farther than the outsider,
who like a snow man was left out: in the cold—alone.

And so,
        in the backward way of our nation,
the yearning for escape,
                our maundering was
the search for the way IN,
              which we outcasts
of the Outcast Club kept trying to invent: the public
password—
         inner sanctum of the circle and city of song!

On the east was the Beet Plant, sugar factory where
the lost battles of the Indians were daily recycled,
sending its smoke signals to the heaven of its dead,
devoured workers,
           or pieces of them: arms,
                   feet,

or bodies caught in the steel maelstroms of the machinery
turning
      turning
            summer's sweet tubers into crystals
white as the snow of a killing blizzard—or the blank
pages of the future where workers lives are erased…

On the west (next to Fargo)—far from the demonic
boilers,
      steam and grime of work,
                  was Ralph's
Corner Bar,
        where Ralph Ristvedt lived, mythical
Norwegian Kilroy invented by jokester Tim Scott,
our Father Black Humor in our time of need
(though in another poem another joker conjured
the rumor of Ralph up, whose soul rides the waves
of imagination like any holy ghost or imaginary
friend): Ralph was a working class time traveler
who knew the Pope and everyone else, even
unimportant people, whose presence was always
near—like God, ubiquitous but more human.

And there, with Ralph for company whom we never
met but always revered because he was free, we tried
to drink up the river—of alcohol.
                  We gathered there for
the illusion given by booze,
                entered the abyss of freedom,
the house of deadly spirits of anesthesia that came
and whirled us away as we sang nonsense inside
the void of the universe,
            whose walls were the four
horizons
        (where always the snow like nightmare drifts
of sugar went on building and burying itself)—
                  we sang

out of the grief, which was like a blue petal frozen in ice—
days lost—
   youth lost—
     we didn't want to feel,
we drank to paralyze our brains and escape the paralysis
of living in an empire that devoured the lives of those
who built it,
    benumbed,
      stuporous,
        mechanic:
an empire dying to die of its own murderous age!

It was then that I once lost my glasses in the snow
in that young time when I was old enough to die in war,
near the river that seemed a frozen road to the house
of the dead, a place built from the bones of crystal birds—
the moon!

    In the translucent night, drunken and alone,
I fell down hunting for my vision, the world blurred,
myopic,
   feeling with my icicle fingers through
the snowy crystals that singed like the sting
of white wasps—
     until my seeing fingers burning
found my glasses,
    but in that cold baptism I lost my sight.

From that clean frozen world I rose with eyes
that couldn't locate my childhood town again:
something had changed,
     crystallized and died within me,
those days of easy praise I always knew were doomed—
buried alive in memory like the world was buried in snow.

I learned what my body had always known:

This brief breathing moment cannot remain the same!—
nor stay long in the small romance of a child's vision,
which to the body whose call and command is change,
means hardly more than a frozen animal in the snow...

And now,
        another snowy vision out of this memory tunnel
appears—
        nearer and less mythic—
                a day at:
the University of North Dakota, Grand Forks,
where I teach, still living on the edge of five dollars,
(while the deans and departmental deities who dine well
are indignant at our discontent, all those Ph.*D*.s), while
the nation is still defined under the sign of confrontation—
between the ruling and the impoverished peoples—
the universe of the poor not mentioned at the University.

An "eternal flame" in the campus forum flutters
in the wind like intellect in its cage, a small bird
locked apart from the world, suspended in the air
on four giant insect legs taller than a door, like
a praying mantis that has by mechanical instinct
devoured reason, while the barren white fury of winter
sweeps across the sleeping earth. The students,
dark shapes in the afternoon, press against the snow.

For most now those times and that war are older than
Ralph Ristveld who long since disappeared into a blizzard
to become more invisible than he always was, joining
somewhere Kilroy, past the horizon we once wished
to escape beyond...
        Even so, they are now old enough
to go to war. They are still young enough not to know
they aren't eternal—they don't know the dangers.
Perhaps their bodies do. They fear poverty the most.

But they are open to the weather—in the weather,
not like the caged ethereal flame on stilts above them,
but like the solar calendar they walk past in the forum:
a hollow half globe that captures the light, marks time
with history's shadow within it. Through the storm
they will hunt their country, and finding it, not love
what they find, though flags fly to claim the wind.
But history's grief unhoused, floating like a split open
sphere, an empty world, on the surf of a snow drift…
belongs to the people…
                    whose hearts have room.

4.

My home town was swept away like a wind constructed city,
built of time's ringing dream tolled out toward the night
of the homeless—or the nightmare of workers hammering
at the gates of our bound past—to make something
out of the nothing we have—

                              ourselves…

    I've been waiting for the bells to announce
    in their deep metallic souls, their chiming depths,
    the tolling and toiling of our needs together!

Far flew those summers free and shimmering in their
complacencies of space…

                    Ghosts out of my nation,
powers out of the cool twilight whirling, dusky shadows
I came to know, that approached with older meanings:
they who had surrendered their labor and lost—
to war or debt, to the gnawing tools that ate their hands,
they who were used up and stepped into the moonlight
and disappeared—
              while high in the east the statue
of a myth faced each dawn, goddess of cold composure
still staring vacant into the brinish deep with her
coin-blank eyes in her aging indifference as her face
is turned from an age of poverty—though they gave
her a face-lift to shine in death-shrine-countenance
each night the citizens dream the empire might be
another country fallen through the stars, or the rain—

    …and in the dark groves the Puritans feared,
    like a trick of moonlight and shadow,
    the guilt of the nation sets up camp—
    the ghosts of Indians or slaves, the many

poor in all colonies, and the bodies
of the Vietnamese still blazing and entranced
between the living and phantasmal governments—
walking nightmares in the napalm forests!

There the kingdom is come whose king is homeless,
like a specter half stepping out of its still smoking skin!

* * * * *

I heard the Sunday bells toll, from my rented room
in Moorhead, calling out the coming of Easter, season of
resurrection as winter thawed into spring and the fire rain
continued to fall over Viet Nam, the bells chiming joy
in the time of our fields of killing—saw the worshippers
arrive wearing the aura of a two thousand year old myth…

And flung my fist into the window where the city,
in its routine of habits, remembered itself without
remembering the world, and in the brilliant morning
I smashed the glass!—
                    to remember myself—
to confirm my own flesh and blood in a somnolent
world unreal:
                    suspended in salvation, the surreal
church goners: to leave my blood's signature on
the shattered window and shatter my nation's
dispassion for another people whose sky was flames,
to learn the wound of my nation's denial cut into
my hand, opening two back knuckles bone-white
when I struck against those damning bells!

Churches,
        banks,
                poverty—
                        decadence,
                                decay,

160

depravation:
>depprivation: privatization…
>>>solipsism:

anger—
>the synonymous segue…
>>bibles of despair!

A word made into a fist or a fist made into a symbol:
the perpetual *NO* of my nation made into a momentary
YES!—
>by small private revolution, incitation of pure rage,
to smash the old world and the reflection of myself
locked in its glass,
>>to vent my human impiety against
those piously fanfaronading faitheaters—while anti-Semitic
Billy Graham commiserated with Nixon—and make a sign
whose memory-scar I still wear on my left hand
(another kind of survival)—
>>>fearless reckless of danger
and therefore dangerous hand unarmed like water…

Fist,
>word,
>>symbol: all three will here be wounded,
and were,
>>and are: all inquiries sustained in the body,
the commune, the call and cry of the Universe.

Remote the morning seemed, out on the street,
the indexes of light ordained by the manifestoes of wealth—
the sacred sleepwalking middle class saints and silences!—
while I was possessed like a hollowed and unhallowed
darkness,
>a wraith of wrath anarchic and chaotic out of
the dissonant and dispossessed past, when I smashed
the window against the claustrophobic sky-line, wanting
to shatter the seraphic light as the glass shards rained down,

even as the church bells cast out their benedictions like vain
birds, wings thin as tin shedding their heavy timbres,
chimes or charms to fly down over the town, like ringing
commands against any unholy quiet attended by the dead
of Viet Nam,
            those ghosts the unwanted congregation.

I saw the glass slivers shiver and shine cold in the sun,
capturing and releasing the edges of colors, as the vista
of the universe for an instant shifted,
                    gyrating down—
fragments of light—
          a world broken—
                  for an instant
before it pulled itself back into a peaceful town
as I thought of the villages torn apart, shredded by
the lazy dog fragmentation bombs—
               10,000
flying razors—
        by Johnson's dictum and dictate: "Unless
the United States has unchallengeable air power, we shall
be hostage to every yellow dwarf with a pocket knife."

The angelic and white Christian hosts from the sky!

Abstract fire! Abstract money—the planes and profits
soar!—
      the cities ablaze!
           Or villages…

The bombs like puffballs we used to snap as children—
far below—seen from the cloud grazing ranges
of the sky.
        And the dreaming child in another country
diving upward into flame!
            The wind sliding over
the silence that remains,

                    gathering up the murdered
voices no one heard—
                while the choirs of salvation
in Moorhead sang toward higher and more rarefied
altitudes than the War Department could reach.

In a nation where all freedoms are defined by
their confusions I wanted a way out of my *in*human
condition: escape…freedom from…primitive…
instinctual…in my youth…romantic rebellion: alone.

I yearned to discover a way into the city which is still
uninvented…

Fancy dancing with my hand, which couldn't later
pay a doctor, I learned how the past, in all its accumulated
anger,
          suddenly flies up, decides without decision
its suffering is enough!
                  And my hand then mourned
in itself,
          in the wound and opened bone of itself, all other
hands secretly dying for the joy of hands—animal hand
hunting its human glove of light, mythic hand hunting
its own myth—to reach out beyond itself—
                        toward…

* * * * *

Hunting my home town.

                Hunting a place name where
the wanderer doesn't belong to the distance, the beggar
to loneliness, the worker to work. Any name would do,
but first the place must be freed—or we who arrive,
citizens of a country fallen through the stars.
As I know now the struggle is old as our ancestors,

163

the memory of their hands in ours, together in all that
lost and still living time organized within our needs.

Hunger compels us, which never came to rest,
like the air knocking at the sea or walking through
the wheat—though we tried to ignore it, send hunger
away like an unwanted guest into the weather,
it remains with us like those we ignore remain,
though poverty become a cliché like the national
anthem. And something more compels us:
necessary to survival: the food we are to each other,
by which we free ourselves from solitary confinement—

Out of the old energies of sleep the ancestral workers
levitate,
      between dark and dawn,
                      approach the city
of light—sheen of asphalt streets empty…
                                   open…

Our collective grief, like a ghost city, shapes itself
within that gray world: the depression that haunts
the country possesses this empty moment—shadow city.
The legacy of debt remains the only property of the poor,
passed on from parent to child, the wages of our labor.

Out of the waste, the history denied which continues
even as we sleep—from the country of the buried horse
to the country of the rusted automobile—from those days
where the wings the sky expelled skidded into earth, from
the frontiers of dusty lightning!—*comes the hint of a cry*—
repeats variations of discontent, but says something
more terrible than the passing of the seasons happened:

   in the wasted seasons the black fires
   consumed each victim alone
   and grief whose language is

powerless fury said in the stirrings
of dry autumn, perhaps in the skeleton
of a dead bush inhabited by no god:
"I whom no one wants may be
the vehicle, the way history burns
through all the denied past,
these lightless flames, but I
who have become alone in time
refuse to be the destination."

And from then to now come hollowed vowels—
from places that never consented to indifference,
where the crime was denied even before
it was committed—the nation's history exiled
to the wind—a vagrant hunger, a weightless
momentum that has forgotten its beginnings,
but is still a need—calling out of the gray world.

Calls to the dreaming child who wanders
the sleeping country…the wilderness of birds
with folded wings in the shape of rocks…who wanders
hunting the river, or the legend of a river beneath dry
thunder that reverberates as if the sky were hardpan.

Who will answer only with the same insistence—that
the nation requires water, the communal language
of the weather…and our own language be liberated…
And between all nations the interstices of the stars
are the same. The silence the same between all stars
whose rays dive thinly into the lakes. The distance
to the stars the same from the reach of all trees,
from all nations like an invisible net that keeps us.

And far within each nucleus of each atom the message
is the exchange of our virtual worlds, a flash ignited
on the horizon!—traveling the edge of the crystal darkness
which crackles and gives something away, the message

165

in matter itself—which is itself energy—in transformation
and flux: cannot be captured in the time-locked vaults—
or sucked into the black hole of the electronic ledgers.

Somewhere between the light of dawn and faint stars,
all these moments of the same moment
                                                            I return to:
turning to turn toward:
                                    my home town: sadly
with these hard eyes.
                                    Dim cities behind my eyes
I see anchored somewhere in the future:
                                                            shadows
attached to air—
                        virtual cities—
                                                ghost cities floating
in the gray tidal wash of dawn,
                                    world calling from
since when,
                        inhabited by our lost phantom selves…

    "In the dream pool I saw
    a transmutation of masks
    like the changing countenance
    of moon and water—with eyes
    black and clear as obsidian
    as if born from the history
    of volcanoes—or the ancient
    fires of war, the depth of a gaze
    that held the panorama of
    night—and into those eyes
    grief and fear like dark wings
    descended toward the ghostly
    stars glazed white as chalk
    in the young brightness of dawn…"

The eyes of the centuries release to the opening day

the visions...
>Workers awaken to invent the world,
without private property, the economies of war!

Our own cities...
>newly fallen through the stars...

we come to: this moment like an opening tunnel of light—
we've come not to be told the earth is owned, not for this
message has the silence waited for the listeners to speak.

"I came...
>I saw...
>>I wept..."
>>>and awakened
and stepped away—
>from my private dispossessions
into a world dispossessed—
>calling from the margins
of vapor between ocean wave and sky, from the borders
of the ghostly unmade world the wind calls
out of the past out of the future—
>we call to ourselves—
and have been calling all this time: out of our origins:

>We've come from the limits of rust and hope,
>morning dew and despair.
>>We have come
>out of our long age of sleep from stone steps
>that descend into the sea, each one a generation.

The elements of the weapons shall adjourn from
neglect and return unbound to the earth.

>The tools

freed at last!

Dale Jacobson .

The money freed from itself:

the fire bird dances over the water—

the energies
unified…

earth becomes,

waters become

oceans become

winds become

words become

work becomes cities become distance becomes

the open cry the dark mouth of the sliver

of the moon becomes the open *C* quiet cry

of night becomes the dawn stepping over

the edge of the world becomes the open grief

the long centuries the far commune the exhausted

circle of ashes becomes the horizons we become

our home becomes our earth voyaging through

the void
vastly:
One…

About the Author

Dale Jacobson's poetry has appeared in numerous journals. His close friendship with Thomas McGrath, whom Adrienne Rich once characterized as "the great Midwestern radical workingclass poet," led to his providing editorship for the definitive edition of McGrath's epic poem, *Letter to an Imaginary Friend*. Jacobson's five previous books of poetry include *Dakota Incantations* (1973), *Poems for Goya's Disparates* (1980), *Shouting At Midnight* (1986), *Hunting My Home Town* (1997), and *Voices of the Communal Dark* (2000), the last two from Red Dragonfly Press known for it fine hand-printed productions. Forthcoming from Red Dragonfly Press is a long poem entitled *A Walk by the River,* which Jacobson describes as "a metaphysical inquiry." He resides in his home state of Minnesota.

Printed in the United States
955100004B

9 781403 360014